STORY OF A MOSQUE IN AMERICA

Dr. Faroque Khan,M.B.(Kmr),M.A.C.P.

Printed in the United States by Cedar Graphics, Iowa.

Distributed by:
Islamic Center of Long Island
835 Brush Hollow Road
Westbury, New York 11590
Phone: (516) 333-3495
Fax: (516) 333-7321
E-Mail: icli@muslimsonline.com
Web site: http://muslimsonline.com/icli

TABLE OF CONTENTS

Shelley and Stephen Limmer
AMJID Participants
Anisa Mehdi
Reporter/Producer for PBS *Religion and Ethics News Weekly*
Dr. Nawal Nour
Sudanese-American, Harvard-trained Ob/Gyn specialist
Marghoob Quraishi
Marghoob Quraishi, a very active member of the Muslim community, is a certified management consultant with vast experience in management.
Bobby and Irwin Rosenzweig
AMJID Participants
Habibullah Saleem
Habibullah Saleem is an educator, writer, consultant, and author of seven books, including those for inspiring and educating our youth.
Frederick A. Smith, M.D.
Physician, Director of Religion and Medicine Course at North Shore University Hospital
Sayyid M. Syeed
Secretary-General, Islamic Society of North America
Michael Wolfe
Michael Wolfe, is author of *The Hajj: An Americans Pilgrimage to Mecca*, and *One Thousand Roads to Mecca*, as well as a books of poetry, fiction and travel writing.

Glossary

DEDICATION

To my parents, Sara and Ghulam Hassan Khan, who taught me the meaning of Islam by practice and example.

To my wife, Arfa, who has been a confidant and life partner for over 30 years.

To our children, Shireen, Seema, Arif, and grandchildren Hassan and Leena who have been a source of great joy and happiness in our lives.

And a very special thank you to Ann Borg for her outstanding service over the years.

WHY THIS BOOK? PREFACE:

"You should bring in more people here to show them you don't make bombs here in the Mosque." This comment by the fire commissioner of Westbury after his visit to Islamic Center of Long Island in early 1990's left an indelible impression on me.

The stereotypes, myths, and misinformation regarding Islam and Muslims, particularly in North America, are common. In fact, one could easily write a book about that, itself.

While Muslims on an individual basis are doing their part in explaining the faith of Islam to non-Muslims, the management at ICLI felt that there need to be an institutional effort to present the true image of Islam which embodies peace, justice, and moderation, with a focus on the role of the Mosque. This book provides that story, a journey which has been fulfilling and challenging.

In various chapters we have described, in detail, the interfaith initiatives, the significance of getting engaged in political discourse, and the election 2000 which was, in my view, a milestone for Muslims.

I have also addressed commonly asked questions, such as "Do Muslims believe in the Prophet Jesus," "Are women treated poorly," "What really happens inside a mosque?"

Being in close proximity of New York City, with its enhanced media presence we have had to deal with crisis, like the World Trade Center bombing, air crashes of TWA Flight 800 and EgyptAir 990. Many useful lessons were learned.

I have devoted chapter 11 to three unique events, highlighting Islam's emphasis on a) education---the very first revelation of the Quran was "IQRA" translated means "Read" (Chap 96) b) tolerance---the comments of the former hostage Terry Anderson are an eye opener and c) the importance of gratitude and thanks for those who do good---the example of Roy Gutmans role in exposing the Serbian genocide against the Bosnian Muslims.

Finally, the remarks of many visitors are, indeed, heartwarming and a sincere thanks and appreciation to all of them.

For Muslims, this book gives a road map of how to accomplish the goals of interfaith dialogue, political empowerment, and how to manage a successful, financially sound Islamic center/mosque in America.

For the non-Muslims, this book will provide an answer to questions that often get asked about Muslims by non-Muslims. As the fire commissioner of Westbury advised, (about a decade back) "Bring more people into the mosque so they know what you do here." This book is an attempt to do just that.

Faroque Ahmad Khan
Long Island, New York
March 2001

1. Shireen Khan, author's daughter, presenting her report (1984).

2. First *Eid al Fitr* congregational prayer at ICLI - Mar. 15 1992.

3. Michael Wolfe with ICLI Sunday School class - Mar 21, 1998

4.
Dr. Hassan Hathout
addressing ICLI
Sunday Adult Session -
Nov 9, 1997

2A

5.
Group of Bosnian refugee students during visit to ICLI.

6. Seven Westbury high school apprentices at their hospital orientation with Mr. John Iannucci (right) and Dr. David Westring, Associate Dean (seated), and Dr. Mohamed Rizvon, Preceptor.

7. George Pataki with members of ICLI on August 14, 1994 at the launch of his Long Island gubernatorial campaign for New York State.

8.
Legislator Roger Corbin and Sr. Rabia Aziz at ICLI - January 10, 1996.

9. Congressman Peter King at the open-house ribbon-cutting ceremony of ICLI on June 5, 1993. Also pictured left to right Nazir Mir, Dr. Arfa Khan (partially hidden), Col. Claude Dixon, Dr. Parvez Mir, Nasir Farooqi, guest, Dr. Safdar Chadda, and Dr. Safia Hameed.

10. New York State Comptroller Carl McCall, highest ranking elected democrat in NYS at ICLI, May 31, 1998.

11. Author with other representatives of the American-Muslim community at the Eighth Annual Prayer Breakfast in the White House on September 14, 2000. Pictured in the middle is Imam Warith Deen Mohammed of the American Muslim Mission, to his left Sayyid M. Syeed, Secretary General of the Islamic Society of North America.

12. Westbury School District (WSD) Superintendent Robert Pinckney (fourth from right) with members of ICLI and elected officials of the school board, Village of Westbury, and NAACP. Mar 12, 1995.

13. Murad Hoffman with ICLI members signing his book *Journey to Makkah*. Nov. 15,1998.

14. Members of Long Island faith based organizations at the Washington Holocaust Museum, with Dr. Arsad Karcic reading a prepared statement. Dr. Karcic had been imprisoned, along with his family, in a Serbian concentration camp. Jan 25, 1995.

15. Lyoma Usmanov, Special Envoy and Designated Ambassador of the Islamic Republic of Chechnya, at ICLI on October 23, 1999.

16. Agha Saeed (Middle), President of the American Muslim Alliance (AMA), with key members of the NYS Chapter of AMA at ICLI Sept. 14, 1997.

17. Dr Frederick Smith, (Right) Director of North Shore University Hospital (NSUH) program *Religion and Medicine,* at ICLI after attending the Friday *Khutbah* followed by a discussion of special needs of Muslim patients. Accompanying Dr. Smith are the physicians in training at NSUH. Jan 28, 2000.

18. Commissioner of Police John Gallagher, along with the top brass of the Police Department, reviewing the various law-enforcement issues with representatives of the Muslim community at ICLI.

19. ICLI representatives with the Editorial Board of *Newsday* at its headquarters in Melville.

20. *Pulitzer* awardee Robert Keeler of *Newsday* explaining how news gets
written and reported.

21. Anthony Marrow, Editor-in-Chief of *Newsday,* at ICLI, April 16, 2000.

22. Rabia Aziz, Hoda Spiteri, Gulal Mayar, Arfa Khan and Nisaa Karim
sharing a lighter moment. Jan 10, 1996.

11A

ﻉﻼﻉﻼﻉﻼ

23. Representatives of ICLI with Cardinal Francis Arinze and MSGR. Donald Beckman on April 25. 2000 at a unique multi-faith meeting titled *Meeting of Minds*

ﻉﻼﻉﻼﻉﻼ

24. Muslim women artists' art exhibition titled :*The Contributions of Women in the Intellectual Tradition of Islam: Past and Present.* From left to right Rishma Ladha (USA), Elinor A. Holland (USA), Sharifah Z. Aljeffri (Malaysia), Rohana Fillipi (Italy), Dr. Habibeh Rahim (Curator/Director), Riffat Alvi (Pakistan), Maryam Zangenh (Iran), Tanja Softica (Bosnia).

12A

25. Attendees at the special three-hour symposium titled *Malcom X-Malik El-Shabazz: His Legacy and Contributions* - February 28, 2001.

26. Mr. Mannie Sweat, President of the Central Westbury Civic Association (CWCA) (on the left in suit) awarding the CWCA Lawn-of-the-Month Award to ICLI. Also pictured left to right Al Haaj Ghazi Khankan, the author, and Mohammed Ahmed.

13A

27. Dr. Tajudeen Kashimawo (brides father) listening attentively at the wedding ceremony.

28. Dr. O.O. Ojutiku and Mrs. Lateef Giwa at the wedding reception.

29. MSGR. Thomas Hartman with ICLI Board members Drs Kauser and Qamar Zaman.

30. Rabbi Jerome Davidson of Temple Beth El and the panelists at the symposium sponsored by AMJID and titled *What It Means To Be A Jew In America. The Way It Was and The Way It Is. How Did We Get There. A Perspective of Three Generations.* June 7, 1998.

15A

❧❧❧❧

Photo–Hamza Byas

31. Rabbi Dovid Weiss discussing the differences between Zionism and Judaism. January 14, 2001.

❧❧❧❧

Photo–Hamza Byas

32. Attendees at the session on Jan 14 2001, included several members of the Hasidic Jewish community.

16A

Chapter 1

BEGINNINGS: THE MOTIVATION FOR FORMING THE CENTER AND SOME EARLY CHALLENGES

"Dad, why can't I have a Christmas tree?"

The concept of ICLI grew out of the concerns of a small group of Muslim families, mostly immigrants who settled in Nassau County in the early 70's. The need to preserve their religious identity, cultural heritage, and desire to educate their children in Islamic principles drew these families together, often on weekends. I was often asked the question by my children, "Dad, all our friends celebrate Christmas and Hannukah. They have decorations and lights; why don't we?" To answer these and other similar questions, a small group comprised of 10-15 children started meeting on weekends. Meetings were initially held in a nursery school in Hempstead, L.I., in basements of private homes, rented church facilities that were often very accommodating to the needs of these "new" immigrants. The Advent Church in Westbury, run by the Quaker Foundation, was particularly accommodating. The assembled group of students were "taught" by parents who volunteered their time. Over a period of time, through word of mouth, more families started to get together and the group realized the need for a permanent home. Thus emerged the concept of the Islamic Center of Long Island; and the property at 835 Brush Hollow Road was purchased in 1984. The small two-story house had an adjoining open piece of land, which was earmarked for the construction of a "mosque." The funds for the purchase of this property came from private donations, mostly from the "core" group of families. ICLI was incorporated as a non-profit entity in April 1982 (*Rajab* 1402) under the provisions of the Religious Corporation Law. The small house on the property was altered to accommodate the needs of the children and adults. The first Friday congregation prayer had three adults participating. I wondered what the future of ICLI would be in the midst of a predomi-

1

nantly non-Muslim neighborhood, with the founding members living at great distances from the center, weekend classes having 15-20 children, Friday gatherings of three, and a bank balance of close to zero. The challenges faced by this small community in New York, how it overcame them, and what was learned in the process are the reasons for this book. We hope the lessons learned from our experience will be of help to others. Over a period of two to three years, the core group began to develop rules and regulations for ICLI. Very few had previous experience or knowledge as to the techniques of managing an Islamic center. The very concept of bylaws for ICLI was felt by some to be an oxymoron - why not just follow the *Quran* and *Sunnah*? After some discussions and consultations, it became clear that an administrative structure was a must if this entity had any chance of success. The group had to deal with the village authorities, obtain permits for construction, pay the bills for utilities, and organize events for the growing community - both children and adults. Thus began the process of development of bylaws for ICLI. Dr. Sultan Hameed was the principal architect for developing these bylaws. In retrospect, this "document" served the community extremely well during several subsequent unexpected, difficult and turbulent times. I recommend that all centers develop bylaws that are suitable for their needs and, even more importantly, adhere to them and update, modify them as the needs and circumstances warrant. Having established some basic rules and regulations for its governance, the group turned its attention to the construction of a mosque that would meet the needs of this small and growing community.

How to Design and Build a Mosque

The majority of the founding members were physicians who, by and large, had little knowledge or experience in the design or construction of a center or a mosque. We needed help, and after making inquiries it became apparent there was no dearth of talent in the community. One just had to reach out and find the appropriately trained personnel. Our community was blessed with the presence of Nazir Mir, an engineer who

2

undertook the task of supervising the construction of an innovative new Islamic Center of Long Island. Advertisements were placed; bids were invited, and several submissions were received. From amongst those submitted, the group felt the design, presentation, and interest of the firm of David Hirsch was the best one, and a contract was signed with the design firm of Hirsch/Danois Architects, New York. Some members questioned the wisdom of having a non-Muslim design a mosque. There were some healthy discussions; opinions were sought from "scholars" here and overseas, and finally the group stayed with the decision. The plans for the building were submitted in January 1988. A building permit was issued in July 1989.

Community Involvement

Over a period of months, as the design and details were being discussed, we invited all members of the community - women and men - to engage in the selection and fine-tuning of the design, and selection of color schemes. We also sought and received the input and comments from neighbors - non-Muslims - whose properties were adjoining ICLI. To the extent possible, their suggestions were incorporated in the design of the plan.

Interaction with Neighbors

Some of the residents in Westbury initially expressed concerns regarding the construction of an Islamic center. In fact, in February 1988 a signed petition was submitted by approximately 90 residents asking the Village of Westbury to refuse a building permit. To address these concerns, the neighbors were invited in February 1988 to review the plans and give suggestions for modification (which several did). A conscious effort was made to keep the neighbors informed about the various stages of construction, and their concerns regarding parking, traffic flow, etc. were given serious consideration. Public hearings were held by the Village of Westbury, at which several neighbors expressed support for the project. An ongoing dialogue was maintained with the Central Westbury Civic Association (CWCA). Several meetings were held and views exchanged regarding parking, community projects, etc. An "Islamic summit" was held on October 7, 1992 between CWCA Housing Committee, a few ICLI trustees, and members of the New Cassel neighborhood. The main concern of CWCA was regarding parking, particularly on Fridays. Following this meeting, several steps were taken to inform members of ICLI about basic parking rules and regulations, and we encouraged ICLI attendees to be sensitive to our neighbors' concerns regarding this issue. The final designs were submitted to the Village Board of Westbury in January 1988. An approval for construction of a minaret was denied, as the height of the minaret did not conform to the village zoning laws. Plans for the rest of the building were approved in July 1989, and the foundation of ICLI was laid on Sunday, December 11, 1988. The founding members were joined by many new members and the leadership of the Village of Westbury. This even received a brief mention in *The New York Times*, and for historical record we reproduce that news item below.

The New York Times - Sunday, December 18, 1988

A First Mosque

Ground was broken last weekend for Long Island's first mosque "from scratch," and Dr. Faroque Khan said the Island's Muslims couldn't be happier. "In the past, Islamic centers in the area have taken what's available, said Dr. Khan, the president of the Islamic Center of Long Island.. "They've bought a church, for example, and modified it." But the mosque that will soon be built on Brush Hollow Road in Westbury is to be the first building on Long Island erected solely as a mosque, Dr. Khan said. The 7,000-square-foot building will be the religious center for about 200 Muslim families who live in Nassau County. Many of those families have a doctor in the house. "Our Islamic center is a Who's Who of physicians," said Dr. Khan, who is chief of medicine at Nassau County Medical Center and whose wife, Dr. Arfa Khan, heads the thoracic radiology department at Long Island Jewish. Dr. Khan estimates that many thousands of Muslims call Long Island home. "Islam is the fastest-growing religion in this country," he said. "There's a great need for awareness about Muslims on Long Island. Our mosque, we hope, will serve as a communication center for our religion." Certain considerations had to be taken into account in building the mosque. "The biggest part is the direction," Dr. Khan said. "We pray toward Mecca. On Long Island that means facing east." The architect had to take that into consideration in the layout, as well as in the construction of the prayer tower. A dome is another important part of a mosque, Dr. Khan said: "It's kind of like saying someone up there is watching over us.'

4

Where is the money coming from? FUND RAISING.

The center was projected to cost over a million dollars. The group had approximately $200,000 available; and in view of the prohibition of usury/interest in Islam, the group could not apply for interest-bearing loans from banks. This, in retrospect, was a blessing in that the group was forced to live and build within its cash reserves and build only what it could pay for. How does one go about raising a million dollars for construction of a mosque in Nassau County?

Some early recollections:

It's, again, useful to emphasize that the group was comprised of professionals – physicians, engineers, businessmen, many of whom were getting established in their professions, buying homes, and caring for young families. Few, if any, had large cash reserves; and since most were immigrants, none had family resources available. This inexperienced young group of Muslims tried every conceivable way of fund raising, which included:

> Monthly Luncheons
>
> This was a pot luck kind of arrangement. While the monies raised were modest, this gathering served the useful purpose of developing cohesiveness amongst the families. They began to identify common goals, shared their experiences, and helped build a momentum towards the anticipated "big event" for fund raising.
>
> Overseas Fund Raising
>
> This method did not work out for our community. In December 1986, I went on an extensive trip to Saudi Arabia, filled out applications with the *Awqaf*, met many individuals and, except for a few small donations from private citizens, returned with the impression that we will be better served raising funds locally in the USA. This, again, turned out to be a blessing, as subsequent

events would show. The monies for the center were generated predominantly from Long Island, and the contributors took a keen interest in the functioning of this center and, in my opinion, is one of the main reasons for the success of ICLI and the development of the rich array of programs and products.

The Big Event - MOMENT OF TRUTH

Having received the building permit and watching the growth and enthusiasm of the community, we decided to have a "big" fund-raising event to finally decide if we had the finances in hand - about a million dollars - to start construction. This event was held at Akbar Restaurant in Roosevelt Field and surpassed everyone's expectations. Within a period of about half an hour, over a million dollars were collected in cash and pledges. This was a great confidence builder, and reinforced a basic principle that individuals will respond to specific goals that are attainable and clearly identified. Several factors, in my opinion, were responsible for this very successful fundraiser -

1. There was a clear need, perceived by the community, for this type of a center in Nassau County.

2. The land was purchased, had been visited and inspected by members. It was for "real."

3. The Model: For most of us looking at abstract drawings made by architects, engineers do not carry the same message as looking at a real model that we had instructed the architect to prepare. This model was available for viewing at all fund raisers, and the members could see and feel and touch the various parts of this planned center. We had the picture of this reproduced on the ICLI brochure, and the visual message of the proposed center was an important element in the success of the fund raising activities.

Reproduced below are pictures of the model:

Ongoing Fund Raising

The experience in fund raising at ICLI has led us to the following methods of ongoing fund raising, so as to maintain a healthy balance sheet for the myriad of operational and capital projects.

1. Weekly Friday Collections: This traditional method is maintained. Collection boxes are placed at strategic locations in the foyer of ICLI, and congregants are reminded to donate generously after the completion of prayers on Fridays.

2. Annual Day: Each summer, the Annual Day is held where the progress of the children's education is assessed. Volunteers and teachers are recognized and each family is expected to contribute between $150 to $200.

3. Annual Event in November: This is the main fundraising event for ICLI. Each November, members, friends and community supporters of the Islamic Center of Long Island (ICLI) congregate for an evening dinner event to assess the Islamic Center's progress, review its programs and raise money for the Center's annual budget. During the course of the gathering, ICLI honors community members who have made outstanding contributions to the Center's work, and recognizes a special guest who has made noble contributions at national and international levels to bettering the understanding and perceptions of Islam - whether through books, personally embracing Islam, developing community interfaith dialogue, or taking a principled moral stand on an important issue.

ICLI has made a conscious and strategic decision to reach out and introduce Islam and Muslims as productive, thoughtful contributors to society. This event helps to accomplish this goal. This gathering of 300-400 individuals has been known for the collegial mix of Jewish, Christian and Muslim community leaders who come together for the evening to celebrate religious diversity and harmony.

Previous events have recognized Salam Al Marayati (1999), Director of Muslim Public Affairs Council; Murad Hofmann (1998), former high-ranking NATO officer and now author from Germany who embraced Islam; Dr. Hassan Hathout (1997) as an author and leading Islamic scholar in the U.S.; Robert Keeler (1997), Pulitzer Prize winning journalist from Newsday; Dr. Laila Al-Marayati (1996), President of the Muslim Women's League, member of the U.S. delegation that traveled to China for the Women's Forum; Monsignor Thomas Hartman (1995), host of the Catholic TV cable channel on Long Island; Abdurahman Almoudi, Executive Director, American Muslim Council; Danny McCue, Editor, Westbury Times; Azizal Al Hibri (1994), Professor of Law, President Karamah, Muslim Female Lawyers for Human Rights. In 2000, ICLI recognized three outstanding women for their contributions – Arab American-Yvonne Haddad, Sudanese American - Dr Nawal Nour and Turkish American – Merve Kavacki. For the year 2001 annual dinner on Saturday, October 20th, the keynote speaker will be author Karen

Armstrong. It's important to schedule the event ahead of time to allow proper planning, advertisement,etc.

The charge per person is $500, and the monies are collected in advance. No fund raising is done during the event. Approximately half of the year's operational ICLI budget is collected during this event.

Having collected enough money to get started, the foundation stone was laid on December 4, 1989. It turned out to be an exceptionally cold and blustery day. In addition to the enthused ICLI members, several members from the Westbury Village Board and neighbors attended this historic event. Soon construction started, and very quickly we realized that the funds allocated would not be sufficient to complete the project. I recall we once reached an almost-zero bank balance and were prepared to stop construction. I made this announcement at the Friday congregation, on July 19, 1991. On Monday July 22, 1991, a member who has chosen to remain anonymous came to my office with four different bank drafts – each for twenty-five thousand dollars. This generous contribution brought to life the *Quranic surah 2:264 - O ye who believe. Cancel not your charity by reminders of your generosity or by injury–like those who spend their wealth to be seen of men.*

During the ensuing years we had several such close calls and challenges. At each juncture the community came through, and after a temporary Certificate of Occupancy was obtained from the village, the facility was made available for Friday congregations etc. During this time we had to deal with Ms. Michelle Depew, who was the building inspector, and she once "closed" the facility due to "code" violations. I mention Ms. Depew here for a very special reason. She was so influenced by her subsequent interaction with the community, that she embraced Islam and later on became a leading advocate and supporter of the community.

Designing ICLI

Project: Islamic Center of Long Island, Westbury, NY.

10

Architect:	Hirsch/Danois Architects, New York, NY (David L. Hirsch, partner-in-charge and senior designer; Mark Alan Stoller, project architect and designer; Marcy McInelly and Jonathan Perlstein, design team).
Client:	Islamic Center of Long Island Program: Design of new mosque including prayer room, multipurpose space, classrooms, offices, and day-care facilities, all situated around a landscaped prayer courtyard. Building Area: (net/gross, square feet) 8,865/9,971.
Cost:	$250/gsf.
Major Materials:	Split-faced concrete block and exterior insulation system, standing seam metal dome cover, steel frame on exterior bearing wall structure, steel-framed dome, plywood-framed column covers, gypsum wallboard with horizontal reglets, gypsum ceiling.
Consultants:	Veldshteyn/Slutsky Associates, mechanical; Albert P. Kung & Associates, structural.
CAD-developed?	No
Architect's Statement:	A trip to the mosques of Isfahan and Shiraz, Iran, was one of the inspirations for this religious and educational center; traditional Islamic features are used in a new, dynamic way to represent their translation into the American context. The vertical wall of the *iwan*, projecting beyond the horizontal front wall of the building, provides entry to a skylit galleria which divides the prayer hall from the multipurpose room. When combined, the two rooms can accommodate approximately 500 worshippers. The *qibla* wall extends beyond the present building boundaries and is planned to enclose an exterior prayer court and reflection pool in a second phase of construction. The lower level of the building contains classrooms and ritual bathing facilities.

"Your permanent Certificate of Occupancy for the Islamic Center of Long Island is approved," Mayor Strada, Village of Westbury, February 8, 1993.

This announcement was made at the completion of a meeting between the Village of Westbury government and two representatives of ICLI, Mr.

Nazir Mir, Project Director, and Faroque Khan, Spokesperson. Finally, after five years of planning, fund raising, and community interaction, the dream of an ICLI on Long Island had become a reality! Thank Allah for His guidance and mercy.

The building of a mosque, designed as a mosque, on Long Island received a fair amount of attention and was reported in *The New York Times*, portions of which are excerpted below:

L.I. Mosque Is Sign of Islam's Community Growth
A New House of Worship Fills Both a Social and a Religious Void.
New York Times, February 25, 1993

At first, there were only three, and they prayed in the basement. Now there are more than 500, and they have moved from a modest house in this suburban village to a mosque across the lawn - finished this month despite a lack of money and the consternation of neighbors who at first did not care much for the faithful in a basement, much less in a mosque in their backyard.

The Islamic Center of Long Island is now an austere presence on a quiet street, just a few miles from muffler shops, pancake houses and churches. It has opened just in time for Ramadan, the Muslim month of fasting, after three years of construction and nine years of discussion among families concerned about the Islamic education of their children.

"Some of our little kids were starting to ask at Christmas time where our trees were," said Dr. Faroque Khan, a founder of the mosque. "We realized that unless we gave them a structure, there were going to be difficulties."

Of the seven mosques on Long Island, the center is the first one built for that purpose rather than placed in a renovated building. That the center was able to raise $2 million for the mosque's construction attests to the growth of the Muslim community in Long Island. Dr. Khan says it is home to 10,000 to 15,000 Muslims, up from only a few thousand 10 years ago.

Muslim communities are similarly growing in New York City, where an ambitious mosque project was recently completed on the Upper East Side, and where Muslims successfully lobbied at City Hall for alternate-side parking for Muslim holy days. Northern New Jersey's first mosque to be built for that purpose opened in Teaneck in 1986.

The mosque here had humble origins. A few families bought a small piece of land in 1984, and ground was broken in 1990. While the mosque was under construction, the basement of a small house on the property was used to hold Koran classes and prayers on Friday, the Muslim holy day.

Ayman Soubani, a doctor from Jordan who worships at the

12

mosque, said it had filled a social void in the community, in which bar-hopping and mixed dancing are forbidden. "Before, there was really no place for social gatherings," he said. "Now we have a place to gather together both for prayer as well as discussions, socializing and learning."

The mosque is intricately designed to reflect a variety of cultures, and awaits the traditional calligraphy on its interior walls. It has no minaret, a tower traditionally attached to mosques from which the calls to prayer are made. "We didn't want to push it," said Dr. Khan. "It is a question of adjustment for the people. But as time goes by, we will get one."

The "adjustment" question first came up in a petition by residents asking the town not to permit the new house of worship. Dr. Khan said he suspected that "people had this image of violence and guns."

The mosque's founders tried to reach out to critics by bringing residents into the planning and by teaching them about Islam.

From Empty Lot to Prayer

"We brought them here and told them that this was the house of God," Dr. Khan said. "Now, we couldn't be more pleased. One man recently told me that this was the best thing that could have happened, because an empty lot that could have been used to sell drugs is now a place of prayer."

Ann E. Sweat, chairwoman of the housing committee for the Central Westbury Civic Association, said about 90 Westbury residents had signed a petition when the land was bought for the mosque, voicing concerns primarily about parking congestion on holidays and Fridays.

"The mosque has worked with a nearby church to ease some of these problems," said Mrs. Sweat, adding, "We now feel that the mosque is a credit to the community. We are 100 percent satisfied."

Most of the mosque's founders are from Kashmir, a territory still in dispute between India and Pakistan. But the mosque now draws Muslims from all around the region, and nationalities range greatly, as do viewpoints on how Islam should be practiced. For example, women pray in the same room as the men in a line directly behind them, as opposed to in another room or behind a partition, as is common in many mosques.

"There are some conservative Muslims from the region who have come and been offended," said Daisy Khan, Dr. Khan's niece and interior designer for the mosque.

Reporter: Jennifer Steinhaure

In 1988 the residents of Westbury had reservations regarding a "mosque" or "Islamic Center." With proper dialogue and communication, the attitude in 1993 is completely different. This was best summarized by Mrs. Ann E. Sweat, Chairwoman of the Housing Committee for Central Westbury Civic

Association, who, responding to questions from Jennifer Steinhaure (*New York Times* reporter) regarding the impact of ICLI in Westbury, said, "The mosque has worked with a nearby church to ease some of the parking problems. We now feel that the mosque is a credit to the community. We are 100 percent satisfied." (*New York Times*, Thursday, February 25, 1993)

Now that the building was built, what would be the role of ICLI in Nassau in Long Island where, of the estimated 1.2 million inhabitants, over half are Catholics, a quarter are Jewish, and the Muslims were estimated to be a few thousand? Our experience in dealing with this issue is perhaps the main reason for writing this book. The stereotypes regarding Islam-Muslims are plentiful.

Ten Common Stereotypes About Islam-Muslims

By and large, non-Muslims, particularly in North America, are very poorly informed about Islam and Muslims. The following are some common myths and stereotypes regarding Muslims.

1. WOMEN: Women have very little, if any rights in Islam. They are treated as second- or third-class citizens.

2. PROPHETS: Muslims follow the religion of Muhammad. They do not believe in Prophets Moses or Jesus.

3. TERRORISM: Islam was spread by the "Sword," and most acts of terrorism are committed by Muslims.

4. ARABS: Most of the Muslims are Arabs.

5. POLYGAMY: Most Muslim men practice polygamy.

6. OBSCURANTISM: Muslims resist acquiring new knowledge, as a result most Muslims remain uneducated and illiterate.

7. HUMAN RIGHTS: Muslims are violent by nature and do not believe or practice human rights.

8. BLACK MUSLIMS: In America black Muslims are followers of Nation of Islam and Lois Farrakhan.

9. DESPOTISM: Muslims are opposed to democracy and they encourage autocratic and despotic monarchs and rulers.

10. CLERGY: Muslims follow the guidance and rulings of their clergy, called Imams.

Search For Imam

We felt that ICLI had to take a proactive role in facing these perceptions and misconceptions head-on, and educate and inform the non-Muslim community. One of the earliest questions raised was: "Who is the Imam of ICLI?" To find a suitable candidate, a search committee was set up and included Dr. Naseem Sharieff, Sr. Rubina Ahmed, Dr. Qamar Zaman, and Dr. Faroque Khan. We advertised for this position, interviewed several candidates and tried to match their skills with the projected needs of ICLI, which we felt fell into the following categories:

1. Religious Needs - leading prayers
2. Interaction and Relationship with the Youth
3. Interaction with Women
4. Responding to Queries from Non-Muslims
5. Dealing with Media - This was very important in view of the location in New York.

So we had a job description and were looking for someone who would meet these requirements. The search committee, over a period of several months, interviewed several candidates, some of whom were very well qualified in some areas. However, we were unable to find a candidate who would have the religious background AND be able to relate to the youth and the women, and represent the community amongst non-Muslims. It was a blessing that the search committee had representation from all segments of the community, and each representative was able to make significant contributions in the evaluation and assessment of the candidates. The search committee, being unable to come up with a clear recommendation, came to the conclusion that perhaps a different model could be tried for ICLI. This resulted in the current structure of the ICLI management, with specific individuals assigned to specific tasks:

Leading Prayers: This task is assigned to Imam Hafez Ahmed, who is a Hafez (can recite entire Quran from memory) proficient in the Arabic language and well-groomed in Sharia.

Communications and Interfaith: For this important job, we were fortunate to recruit Al Hajj Ghazi Khankan. His multilingual communication skills, engaging personality, and previous contacts in the communications world made him an excellent candidate for this position. Thus, all inquiries from non-Muslims, lay organizations, TV, radio, are directed to Al Hajj Ghazi Khankan.

Spokesperson: To give a clear, unambiguous message during events of major significance, whether they deal with incidents of terrorism, natural disasters, accidents - TWA Flight 800, EgyptAir 990 crash - a single individual was designated for this assignment. It's been a learning experience, and elsewhere I will summarize the experience gained in discharging this responsibility. (See Page 81)

Educational Curriculum: These would be handled via the Education Committee and, on a regular basis, the curriculum for the students and the program for adults get updated and revised. While the composition of this key committee keeps changing, the steady and professional guidance provided by Professor Sultan Hameed has been invaluable. Professor Hameed's background as a faculty member at the State University of New York at Stony Brook, and his devotion to the activities of ICLI have made his contributions invaluable.

So, in essence, the management team of ICLI is made up of a group of individuals whose job descriptions are geared towards their professional strengths. Few are on the paid staff, while the majority work on a voluntary basis.

Chapter 2

GOVERNANCE AND ADMINISTRATION:
BOARD OF TRUSTEES , EXECUTIVE COMMITTEE

One of the main reasons, in my opinion, for the success of ICLI has been the establishment of a constitution and bylaws, which have served the community extremely well. Over a span of 16 years, ICLI has had a relatively smooth transition of management eight times. This has resulted in bringing in new ideas, diverse management styles and, at times, resolution of "crisis" that have been resolved primarily due to the existence and adherence to the bylaws.

For any Islamic center, I strongly suggest that they consider developing bylaws, amend them based on the changing needs, and adhere to the rules and regulations. I will reproduce some portions of the ICLI bylaws and highlight some key areas that have served the community well.

ARTICLE II: AIMS AND OBJECTIVES

ICLI shall be a non-profit, religious organization within the meaning of Section 501(c)(3) of the Internal Revenue Code, incorporated in the State of New York. The basic purpose of ICLI shall be to serve Muslims and to help them achieve their way of life as idealized in the teachings of Islam. Towards these goals ICLI shall:

- *organize and establish religious, educational, cultural, and social services for Muslims;*
- *cooperate with other Muslim organizations in the tri-state area and elsewhere;*
- *promote cooperation and understanding with people of different faiths.*

ARTICLE III: MEMBERSHIP

Any Muslim of voting age accepting the provisions of this constitution and the bylaws shall be eligible to become a member of ICLI. A

17

Muslim is a person who believes and declares that there is no one to be worshipped except Allah, and that Muhammad (P.B.U.H.) is His final messenger and prophet.

ARTICLE IV: ORGANIZATION

ICLI shall be organized through the following bodies:
- A. *The General Body*
- B. *The Executive Committee*
- C. *The Board of Trustees*

<u>Section 1. The General Body</u>

The General Body shall be composed of ICLI Members as defined in the bylaws.

<u>Section 2. The Executive Committee</u>

- A. *The Executive Committee shall consist of five elected ICLI members; namely, President, President-Elect, Vice-President, Secretary, and the Treasurer.*
- B. *Both <u>men and women</u> shall be represented on the Executive Committee.*
- C. *The Executive Committee shall be advised by the Board of Trustees as set forth in the bylaws.*

<u>Section 3. The Board of Trustees</u>

The ICLI Board of Trustees shall consist of the Immediate Past-President of the Executive Committee, Life Members, Contributing Members, and Elected Members.

Who can become a member?

This requires a written application, payment of prescribed dues, and approval by the Executive Committee. Membership begins on January 1st every year. Annual dues are determined by the Executive Committee.

Role of the Executive Committee

- • Implement the ICLI constitution.
- • Plan, manage, and execute the various outlined objectives.

18

- Carry out policies and decisions of the Board of Trustees.
- Establish procedures for routine functioning.
- Appropriate funds for various activities.

Who is eligible for election to the Executive Committee?

Very, very important. Must have completed at least three consecutive years of membership.

Election Procedure:

First, a Nominating Committee is established by the Board. This committee is composed of:

1. Chairperson of the Board - chairs the Nominating Committee, as well.
2. President-Elect of Executive Committee.
3. Three members from the Board of Trustees.
4. Two General Body members elected by the Board of Trustees.

Both <u>men and women</u> shall be represented on the Nominating Committee. The Executive Committee serves for a two-year period.

Who gets to vote?

All persons who have been ICLI members in good standing for at least one year. Majority vote decides the election.

What's the function of the Board of Trustees?

1. Long- and short-term planning of ICLI in regard to its finances.
2. Advise the Executive Committee on major issues and policy matters.
3. Publish summary reports of activities in the *ICLI Newsletter*.
4. Meet with the Executive Committee at least twice a year.

The Executive Committee establishes standing committees to address:

1. Education
2. Fund Raising
3. Public Relations

4. Social and Cultural Affairs

5. Planning and Development

I have highlighted some of the areas that I feel have been very beneficial for the growth, continuity, and vitality of ICLI. Setting some rules as to the voting eligibility (one-year membership), eligibility to contest election (three years of continuous membership), and ensuring representation of both women and men on the Nominating and Executive Committees have provided a mechanism for ensuring the representation of the various constituencies of ICLI.

Chapter 3

EDUCATIONAL PROGRAMS: CHILDREN, ADULTS – LIMITATIONS AND FUTURE POSSIBILITIES

By
SULTAN HAMEED, Ph.D.
Professor of Marine Sciences
State University of New York at Stony Brook
Chairman, Education Committee, ICLI

THE SUNDAY SCHOOL

The Islamic education of children was the primary motivation for the formation of the Islamic Center, so a Sunday school has been a permanent feature of the Center from the start. The basic challenge of the Sunday school has been to provide meaningful education to children in about three hours a week. In the early phases of the Islamic Center the school consisted of about 20 students and two teachers. As the Muslim community grew on Long Island, so did the enrollment in the school. At the start of the year 2000, 410 students, ranging from 4 to 17 years in ages, were enrolled in the school, taught by 17 teachers.

Because of the limitations in space in the Center, the children have been divided into six groups in accordance with the grade they attend in their regular schools, as follows:

Sunday School Class	Grade Levels in School
A	Kindergarten and 1
B	2, 3
C	4, 5
D	6, 7
E	8, 9
F	10, 11, 12

The children attending our school represent the ethnic and cultural diversity of the Muslim population in Nassau County. About ninety percent of the children are from immigrant families from Pakistan, India, Egypt, and Afghanistan. There is a broad range of interpretations of Islam to which the families subscribe. A major theme in the lives of our students is the tension between the parental culture rooted in their home countries and the Americanization of the children's attitudes.

Within this framework the Islamic Sunday school focuses on a few major principles to accomplish its mission. These may be summarized as follows:

- Faith in Islam is the central principle of our lives; it defines our identity.
- Our living must be illuminated by our faith.
- Moral values are the foundation stones on which we build our personal, family and social lives.
- The Sunday school aims to provide the children with a happy experience of the Muslim community.

The school begins at 9:30 every Sunday morning with an assembly of students and parents. The theme of the assembly is *Al-Fatihah*, its recitation, its meaning and the purpose it imparts to our lives. The assembly is followed by three periods of 45 minutes each, with a recess of half an hour after the second period. Each class has a prescribed set of textbooks for the three periods. Four major strands can be identified in the curriculum of our school. They are presented at each level, but the pedagogy is modified to suit the age of the students. These are:

Basic Beliefs
The Five Pillars
The Quran
The Prophet (peace be upon him)

With very young children, the basics of these four topics are taught through description and repetition. For older children, the school aims to present Islamic principles as a rational set of beliefs. Teenage students are encouraged to participate in class discussions, and to use their reasoning faculties with guidance from the teachers. One period for Class F (the oldest group) is set aside for open discussion, where the students are encouraged to bring up any question that may be of interest to them

22

for a free and uninhibited discussion.

As the Muslim community in the United States has matured and grown, two developments have helped improve the quality of teaching in the Sunday school. One is that a number of Islamic textbooks have been published, written specifically for American students. The second is that young men and women who grew up in the United States have become available to teach in the school. Although most are not trained teachers, their greater facility in communicating with the children has helped the school.

The Education Committee of the Islamic Center manages the Sunday school. Drawing upon the talents of the members of the committee, the Sunday school has systematically moved towards a more professional organization with respect to record keeping, class discipline, and quality of teaching.

SUNDAY PROGRAM FOR ADULTS

Parallel with the children's classes is an educational program for adults every Sunday morning, lasting for three hours. It is designed to be a forum for community discussion on all questions of interest. Its featured topics include discussion of the *Quran* and the *Hadith*, social, economic and political challenges facing the community, women's rights, marriage, parenting, personal health, affairs of Muslims living in different parts of the world, etc. Visitors from outside the Muslim community also speak frequently at this forum. These include public officials, journalists, and representatives of other faiths. The Sunday program for adults also acts as a "Book Club" where significant current books are discussed. Members of the community generally present the reviews. The books being discussed are available for purchase at the Islamic Center. To give an idea of this activity, the books reviewed at the Center in the year 1999-2000 are listed below:

1. *Cultural Forces in the World Today* by Ali Mazrui.
2. *The Bounty of Allah* by Aneela Arshed.
3. *Jerusalem, One City Three Faiths* by Karen Armstrong.
4. *Jinnah, Pakistan and the Islamic Identity* by Akbar Ahmed.

23

5. *Struggling to Surrender* by Jeffrey Lang.
6. *The Meccan Crucible* by Farid Zakaria.
7. *The Conference of the Birds* by Fariduddin Attar.
8. *Terrible Beauty* by Peter King was reviewed by the author who is a US Congressman from Nassau County.

The wide range of topics and speakers ensures the presentation of a variety of views in this forum. The presentations are followed by a discussion, which is free and almost always lively.

The Sunday adult sessions at ICLI have evolved, over a period of time, into a very unique forum, providing the attendees an opportunity, over a three-hour period, to review some current, at times controversial, issues. Also, this platform gives ICLI a venue for inviting visiting dignitaries and politicians, particularly at the time of elections.

We have also used this forum to highlight a particular issue that often gets overlooked. For example, the issues of *End-of-Life Care* and *Organ Transplantation* were discussed with a transplant surgeon, an ethicist, and a Muslim scholar. The attendees got state-of-the-art information regarding these very relevant and contemporary issues.

At other times we have invited news personnel for in-depth discussions. Mr. Anthony Marrow, Editor of *Newsday*, heard firsthand the concerns Muslims have regarding the reporting in the print media. We acknowledged the marked improvement *Newsday* has shown during the past decade in reporting regarding Islam and Muslims.

Another feature worth mentioning is the symposia we have had during these Sunday sessions, highlighting the contributions of various Muslims from different parts of the world. Syed Ahmed Khan's contributions in the social, intellectual and political development of Indian Muslims were reviewed. We feel that in view of the multi-ethnic, multi-cultural composition of Muslims in America, it's important to have such sessions so that various groups learn about the contributions of different societies.

During the *Black History Month* in February 2001, ICLI organized a symposium celebrating the life and contributions of Malcolm X – Malik El-Shabazz. An overflow crowd of Muslims and non-Muslims heard from speakers who had known this unique man, personally, or were deeply touched by his contributions and legacy. While the movie about Malcolm X presented an aspect of his life, we at ICLI developed the program with a focus on his message as a universalist, a defender of human rights, and a man who held his mother, wife and daughter in great esteem. In particular, we focused on the last year of Malik El-Shabazz's life when, after his pilgrimage to Mecca to perform the *Hajj* in 1964, he returned and preached brotherhood and equality for all. In the short span of 11 years (from the time of his release from prison to his assassination), Malcolm left a lasting legacy. This session was extremely educational, particularly for the immigrant Muslims.

Excerpts of this symposium were the subject of an article in *Newsday*, which is reproduced below.

My advice for communities, particularly the new and developing Islamic centers and mosques, is to develop an adult education program tailored to local needs and environment.

Newsday
Monday, February 19, 2001 – Page A4
Malcolm X Found Fruit in Islam
LI mosque examines faith's effect on him
By Erik Holm
Staff Writer

On a day when hundreds of Muslims usually gather to meet and pray under the gold dome of their mosque, the members of the Islamic Center of Long Island threw open their doors yesterday for a wide-ranging discussion of the life of Malcolm X.

The three-hour panel was the Westbury mosque's center-piece for its celebration of Black History Month and included several speakers who argued that the influential Muslim convert – who they also called by the name he adopted after a trip to Mecca, El-Hajj Malik El-Shabazz – was still misunderstood by much of society nearly four decades after his death. The anniversary of his assassination is Wednesday.

The panelists also argued that popular portrayals of Malcolm cast him as a man filled with hate, a portrayal that Anna Mohammed, a teacher from the Roosevelt school district, said was incorrect.

"His was a human reaction to a subhuman condition," Mohammed said. "It is impossible to hate....and still be concerned about the conditions that your neighbors are living under." Others emphasized Malcolm's role in international politics and how he brought the civil rights struggle to an international stage with two trips to the Middle East and a number of African countries. But the main reason for organizing the panel, said Ghazi Khankan, the director of interfaith affairs for the Islamic center, was to discuss the influence of Malcolm's religion on his teachings in the final months of his life.

It was after his 1964 pilgrimage to Mecca, the holiest of sites for Muslims, that Malcolm's philosophy evolved fully, Khankan said.

"We wanted to talk about how Islam affected his life and transformed him from what he was into that great human being," Khankan said.

Born Malcolm Little in 1925, he said in his celebrated autobiography that his youth was wasted. His life of petty crime ended in 1946, when he was arrested for burglary and sentenced to 10 years in prison. While there, he discovered the teachings of the Nation of Islam, led by Elijah Muhammad. When released from prison, he became an eloquent spokesman for the organization, and often criticized civil rights leaders for advocating integration into white society instead of pushing for independent black institutions.

In 1964, he resigned from the Nation of Islam after learning that Muhammad planned to have him assassinated, and formed a separate Islamic movement whose stated goals included working with the same civil rights leaders he had criticized in his earlier years. But it wasn't until his trip to Mecca later that year, several panelists said yesterday, that Malcolm completed his political and spiritual transformation.

"He became a humanist who wanted harmony between the races, as compared to his anti-white rhetoric before he came to Mecca," said Khankan.

Malcolm was assassinated February 21, 1965 by gunmen affiliated with the Nation of Islam. But in the months following his pilgrimage, panelist Seema Khan said yesterday, "he opened the doors of American society to show not only what a Muslim could be, but what an African-American could be."

27

Historic visit of the Nassau County legislators to ICLI on January 10, 1996.

Alphonse Campbell, Robert Hylton, Ann Sweat, Gil Noble, Mannie Sweat, Faroque Khan, at the Malcolm X-Malik El Shabazz symposium. Feb 18, 2001.

Chapter 4

A WAKE-UP CALL AND THE START OF INTERFAITH DIALOGUE
"Do Muslims believe in Jesus Christ?" - Dr. Roger Bone.

This question was asked in a hotel lobby in Amman, Jordan, during a break from a medical conference while Roger Bone and I were reviewing our impressions from our visit to Amman, Jordan, in 1986. We were visiting Jordan to deliver a series of lectures on Pulmonary Medicine as guests of Dr. Naif Sliman, Chief of Pulmonary Diseases in the Amman Medical School, and his colleagues.

This question represented an eye-opener, wake-up call for me. Dr. Roger Bone, at that time, was one of the most accomplished academic physicians in the USA, even worldwide. His work in various aspects of lung diseases was widely recognized, and he was the Chairman of a major medical school in Chicago, USA, at that time. If an individual of Dr. Bone's intellectual and academic stature was unaware of Muslims' perspectives regarding the Prophet Jesus Christ, what was the understanding of the general population in the USA? One would assume very little.

The answer to Dr. Bone's question was very easy. I shared with Dr. Bone the teachings in *Al Quran* regarding Prophet Jesus, in that Jesus is in fact regarded as one of the five greatest prophets of history - the others being Noah, Moses, Abraham, and Muhammad (Peace be upon them all). No less than 11 chapters of the Quran (out of 114) mention Jesus or his teachings. In fact, one of the chapters is called Maryam (Mary, Chapter 19, Mother of Jesus). The *Quran* does not question the virgin birth, and talks of it as one of the signs of Allah's ultimate power, and describes Jesus as a word from God, not the word of God.

The virgin birth of Jesus is described in the *Quran*, Chapter 19, Ayah's 16-34.

16. *Relate in the Book*　　　　　*When she withdrew*
(The story of) Mary,　　　　　*From her family*
　　　　　　　　　　　　　　　　　To a place in the East.

17. She placed a screen
    (To screen herself) from them;
    Then We sent to her
    Our angel, and he appeared
    Before her as a man
    In all respects.

18. She said: "I seek refuge
    From thee to (Allah)
    Most Gracious: (come not
    near)
    If thou dost fear Allah."

19. He said: "Nay, I am only
    A messenger from thy Lord,
    (To announce) to thee
    The gift of a pure son."

20. She said: "How shall I
    Have a son, seeing that
    No man has touched me,
    And I am not unchaste?"

21. He said: "So (it will be):
    Thy Lord saith, "That is
    Easy for Me: and (We
    Wish) to appoint him
    As a Sign unto men
    And a Mercy from Us":
    It is a matter
    (So) decreed."

22. So she conceived him,
    And she retired with him
    To a remote place.

23. And the pains of childbirth
    Drove her to the trunk
    Of a palm tree:

She cried (in her anguish):
"Ah! Would that I had
Died before this! would that
I had been a thing
Forgotten and out of sight!"

24. But (a voice) cried to her
    From beneath the (palm tree):
    "Grieve not! for thy Lord
    Hath provided a rivulet
    Beneath thee;

25. "And shake towards thyself
    The trunk of the palm tree;
    It will let fall
    Fresh ripe dates upon thee.

26. "So eat and drink
    And cool (thine) eye.
    And if thou dost see
    Any man, say, "I have
    Vowed a fast to (Allah)
    Most Gracious, and this day
    Will I enter into no talk
    With any human being."

27. At length she brought
    The (babe) to her people,
    Carrying him (in her arms).
    They said: "O Mary!
    Truly an amazing thing
    Hast thou brought!

28. O sister of Aaron!
    Thy father was not
    A man of evil, nor thy
    Mother a woman unchaste!

29. But she pointed to the babe.
    They said: "How can we

Talk to one who is
A child in the cradle?"

30. He said: "I am indeed
A servant of Allah:
He hath given me
Revelation and made me
A prophet:

31. "And He hath made me
Blessed wheresoever I be,
And hath enjoined on me
Prayer and Charity as long
As I live:

32. "(He) hath made me kind

To my mother, and not
Overbearing or miserable;

33. "So Peace is on me
The day I was born,
The day that I die,
And the Day that I
Shall be raised up
To life (again)!"

34. Such (was) Jesus the son
Of Mary: (it is) a statement
Of truth, about which
They (vainly) dispute.

This question from my friend, Dr. Bone, convinced me that one of the major tasks for Muslims in North America was to explain the fundamentals of Islam to non-Muslims in North America. Over a period of time, as the community and ICLI as an organization developed and matured, we made a deliberate and conscious effort to engage non-Muslims, particularly of the Abrahamic faith, in a meaningful dialogue.

The following is our experience with interfaith dialogue.

DIALOGUE WITH CATHOLICS

We approached Monsignor Tom Hartman at the Diocese of Rockville Centre where Monsignor Hartman is the Director of popular radio and television programs for the diocese. Monsignor Hartman was extremely receptive, and over a period of several years invited Al Haaj Ghazi Khankan to make regular presentations on his TV shows. To present the women's perspective, he invited Sister Sanaa Nadim, Muslim Chaplain at the University of Stony Brook, to review and present various issues dealing with women in Islam.

In this manner we were able to engage and reach a very large population of Christians, in particular Catholics in Long Island, New York. Monsignor Hartman showed a very keen interest in learning about Islamic teachings, emphasized common features, invited comments from us when he was preparing his book *How Do You Spell God?* I felt like Monsignor Hartman was saying to his audience, "Look, this new group of Muslims has arrived in Long Island. There are lots of common features in our faiths, and I would like you to pay attention to what they have to say."

The Telicare TV station, in addition to regular appearances by Al Haaj Ghazi Khankan and Sister Sanaa Nadim, put together special programs regarding Islam and Muslims. I recall on January 10, 1996, we prepared a special segment titled *Islam's Contributions to Civilization* and showed some of the contributions in architecture, medicine, astronomy, mathematics, etc.

Another unique event which developed, as a result of this interaction, was an interfaith coalition visit to Washington, D.C. to speak to Congress about the situation in Bosnia. This was done on January 25, 1995, and reproduced below is the description of this trip by Monsignor Thomas Hartman in his newsletter.

L.I. Religious Leaders Visit Congress
Reported by Fr. Tom Hartman
Washington, DC:

On January 25, 1995 an interfaith coalition of Muslim, Catholic, and Jewish leaders went to Washington, D.C. to speak to Congress about the situation in Bosnia.

I want to share a story with you that is very painful. It is a story that I wish I did not have to tell you. It is a story about genocide.

On January 25th, we went to Washington, D.C. to visit the House of Representatives and the Senate. We also went to the Holocaust Museum with some priests, rabbis, members of the Muslim community and Bosnia citizens.

We were all made harshly aware of the genocide occurring in Bosnia. We rallied together. We had a common cause to present to Congress about the horrific situation in Bosnia and how action needs to be taken. This group of spiritual leaders was unanimous in decrying genocide and calling for disarmament. Yet, on the other hand, as we wrestled with the question of lifting the arms embargo, our group wondered whether we, as religious leaders, could sanction the use of arms.

32

As we dialogued, a 32-year-old Bosnian doctor spoke. He lived in Sarajevo with his parents and his brother, who is also a doctor. In 1992, when the Serbian troops captured Sarajevo, he and his family were placed in a concentration camp. They watched their fellow Muslims raped, mutilated and killed in public. After a reporter from Newsday covered the story about these atrocities, the Serbs relented and released some of those confined in the prison camps. Unfortunately, only five camps were closed and over 100 continued operation.

A 70-year-old woman, tears streaming down her face, spoke to me about how soldiers came up to her daughter, pointed a rifle to her head and killed her.

Her two sisters were captured, placed in concentration camps and raped repeatedly. Nine of her relatives have been executed. How could we sit back and allow this to happen? The Bosnians gave us this perspective: imagine that your entire family lives on a block. The first day troops come to the first house and kill all the people. The second day, the same thing happens in the second house, and then the same on the third day. What would you do if you were living in the fourth or fifth house?

We walked away with an even heavier heart, saddened to know that 250,000 people have been killed, 50,000 women have been raped, 200,000 people are homeless and 1,200 mosques and churches destroyed.

Monsignor Hartman and other members of the diocese have visited ICLI, interacted with the group and participated at several annual dinners. Many of the ICLI members participated in the annual fundraising telethon of Telicare.

DIALOGUE WITH THE NATIONAL COUNCIL OF THE CHURCHES OF CHRIST IN THE USA (NCCC)

Sayyid M. Syeed, Secretary General of the Islamic Society of North America asked me and the Islamic Center of Long Island to represent them at an important meeting with the NCCC leadership. This was my first formal exposure to this large and influential Christian group. The meeting was held on Thursday, October 30, 1997 at the headquarters of NCCC in New York City. The meeting lasted over two hours. Highlights are reproduced below.

33

The Rev. Dr. Joan Brown Campbell, General Secretary of the National Council of Churches, gave a brief overview of the NCC, which represents 33 member churches world-wide, and has a membership of 52 million. She welcomed the opportunity of meeting the representatives of the Muslims and looked forward to a continuing dialogue.

Mr. David Weaver, Acting Director of the Middle East Office, presented a report of the findings of the NCC official delegation to the Middle East.

After the formal presentation, there was a frank discussion for over an hour, with a focus on how the NCC and Muslims in the USA could build up on this initial contact. I was pleased to note that the NCC is planning to distribute two brief, introductory, 30-page books (written by Muslims) to its members, and follow this up with other written material dealing with how to dialogue.

I got the distinct impression that NCC wants to continue its dialogue with Muslims and develop strategies for joint action in areas of mutual concern. An example of this would be the current bill in Congress dealing with the issue of sanctions against countries which persecute Christians. The NCC is opposed to this bill for obvious reasons.

Ms. Campbell was subsequently quoted in the *New York Sunday Times* of December 21, 1997 regarding NCCC's position on the bill that was under review in the Congress. She stated:

There is reason to be concerned with this overly muscular Christianity that is being persecuted. That's got some history to it. When Christians act like their faith is pre-eminent, it can create problems. I hate to use this example because it's extreme, but if you look at the Nazi regime, you see in it a philosophy of Christian superiority.

The emphasis on persecuting Christians, suggests Campbell, is theologically arrogant.

We are equally concerned about persecution of any faith.
If we, as Americans, are not more careful, we will create
a more repressive situation for Christians.

At the meeting of October 30, 1997, I met Dr. Bert F. Breiner, Co-director of Interfaith Relations for NCCC and the prime mover of meaningful dialogue between NCCC and Muslims. Dr. Breiner has been involved in Christian-Muslim relations, both in the US and overseas, for over 22 years and has taught Islamic studies at the Sally Oak College and the University of Birmingham in England. He contributed to the *Encyclopedia of Islam in the Modern World* and has authored a number of articles on Christian-Muslim relations. ICLI took advantage of the vast experience of Dr. Breiner. He was invited on several occasions to address the members at ICLI, and to the annual fund-raising dinner. We continue to explore further avenues for an ongoing exchange with the NCCC, such as the exchange of students and young adults. Members from ICLI participated in the conference titled *From Conflict to Cooperation - Christian-Muslim Relations in America* organized under the leadership of Dr. Breiner and held in March 1999 in New York City.

TRIALOGUE IN FAITHS

While we found the exchange with individual groups of Catholic and Protestants very informative and useful, we felt that we needed to get the groups together, and chose to do so by focusing on a very contemporary and relevant issue dealing with end-of-life care issues. This three-hour symposium was held at ICLI on November 7, 1999 and titled *Muslim-Christian Perspectives Focused on Contemporary End-of-Life Issues.* The participants were - <u>Panelists:</u> Bert F. Breiner, Co-Director, Interfaith Relations, National Council of Churches; Monsignor Alan J. Placa, Catholic Health Services of Long Island; Feisal Abdul Rauf, American Sufi Muslim Association, New York City, NY; and John Travers, M.D., Chair, Ethics Committee, Mercy Hospital, Rockville Centre, NY; <u>Moderator:</u> Faroque A. Khan, M.B., M.A.C.P., Spokesperson, Islamic Center of Long Island. We used the case-based study method and presented the histories of: *Elderly Patient with Pneumonia and Multi-organ Failure* and *Patient in a Persistent Vegetative State.*

During the very lively and informative discussion the audience, comprised of Muslims and Christians, heard a perspective on issues like: *Pain Control Vs Euthanasia; Life Support - Indications for Initiating and Removing in Elderly Patient; Do Not Resuscitate, Autopsy, Living Will; Conflict Resolution;* and *Definition of Death - What is "Soul?"*

In summary, in our Christian-Muslim dialogue we have learned a lot from each other, developed new friendships and a level of comfort so that we can address issues of mutual concern.

Chapter 5

MUSLIMS UNDER SEIGE:
BEGINNING OF COMMUNITY INTERACTION

"Attacks on U.S. Muslims Surge Even as Their Faith Takes Hold."
New York Times, August 28, 1995, page 1.

The 1993 World Trade Center bombing was an unfortunate event that linked Muslims and domestic terrorism in the USA in the minds of many Americans. This event devastated the efforts of American Muslims to show the good face of Islam.

On April 19, 1995, the day of the Oklahoma City bombing, many American television stations indicated that "Islamic fundamentalists" were the prime suspects. We later learned that Timothy J. McVeigh and Terry L. Nichols, American-born white men, were driven by a religious fervor to commit this crime, but the damage from April 19th coverage was done. There were widespread repercussions against Muslims, acts that included the burning of mosques, vandalism, and attacks against Muslims. In the three days after the Oklahoma City bombing, there were 222 recorded attacks against Muslims - ranging from spitting on women wearing shawls to death threats, to shots fired at mosques, to a fake bomb thrown at a Muslim day-care center (*New York Times*, August 28, 1995).

It was in this background and mind set that the members of ICLI were trying to establish the center in Westbury, Long Island. In a deliberate and planned manner we chose to get the neighboring community involved in ICLI from the beginning. After purchasing the property on 835 Brush Hollow Road in 1984, and as the plans for the construction of the mosque were being worked on, we invited the immediate neighbors (all non-Muslims - Christians) to review the plans with us. We explained the concept of the mosque and the importance of the dome and the Minaret. Many questions were answered, and several suggestions of the neighbors were incorporated; for example, one neighbor suggested that the trees and shrubs between her property and ICLI be of a particular height. This was incorporated. We explained the time schedule of the construction phase, the likely impact that would have and, in short, prepared our neighbors as much as possible. The plan for the Minaret was also dropped.

OPEN HOUSE

Once the construction phase was completed, we wanted to "officially" welcome our neighbors. To do that, we formed a committee consisting of key members of the Central Westbury Civic Association and other prominent activists from the community. Some of the individuals who played a key role in this included retired Colonel Claude Dixon, Mrs. Ann Sweat, and Mr. Mannie Sweat, Mr. John Bennett, Ms. Lorraine Read, and several members from ICLI. Over a period of several weeks a plan was prepared for the open house. In addition to the neighbors, the following were invited: 1) clergy from various denominations in Westbury and New Cassel, 2) the Mayor and village trustees, 3) the Superintendent of Buildings, 4) the County Executive, 5) the Westbury School Board, 6) the Police Commissioner, and 7) media and TV personnel.

The open house was held on Saturday, June 5, 1993. The flavor and tone of the day's events is reproduced in news articles in *Newsday* on June 6th and the *Westbury Times* on June 17, 1993.

Mosque Opens Doors To Neighbors
By Yolanda Rodriguez
Newsday, Sunday, June 6, 1993

Robert Hatcher admired the calligraphy in the Korans that were displayed at the Islamic Center of Long Island in Westbury.

"The writing is very beautiful," Hatcher said to Safia Hameed, a mosque member, about the Arabic script. "It must be very difficult."

Hameed agreed, and then explained that Urdu is her native language and that Arabic was the language of prayer. "We feel we are here in this community," she said in an interview, "and we want to be part of this community."

The open house was a chance to meet the neighbors, heal old disputes, and dispel recent stereotypes of Muslims as terrorists.

"We hope that people understand the religion and its followers," said Dr. Faroque Khan, a spokesman for the center.

Such was the sentiment displayed yesterday at the mosque on Brush Hollow Road, where more than 100 peo-

38

ple walked through, admired the clear, clean white walls of the prayer room, nibbled on food, and marveled at gold-edged Korans and brightly colored prayer mats. As part of bringing together the Muslim and non-Muslim communities, neighbors helped organize the event, which also included a health fair.

Mosque member Ghazi Khankan, after greeting visitors by offering to write their names in Arabic on a card, said, "We want to get to know our neighbors. People drive by and see the building with the green dome. They wonder what we do inside. We thought this would be good. In this day of communications, a lack of it creates fear and ignorance.

"Muslim houses of prayer are really open to anyone to come in. Anyone can come in to ask questions . . . as long as they are dressed decently," Khankan said.

Recently, mosque neighbors complained about parking when people came to worship. To demonstrate a spirit of cooperation, the mosque last month celebrated the Muslim holiday, Eid ul-Adha, commemorating Abraham's offer to sacrifice his son, with 6,000 people at Bethpage State Park instead of the mosque.

Mosque Feted With Open House
By Danny McCue
The Westbury Times, **Thursday, June 17, 1993**

Despite a persistent rain, mosque members and local residents came together for an open house June 5 to celebrate the grand opening of the Islamic Center of Long Island.

The afternoon-long event, held with the assistance of the New Cassel and Central Westbury Civic Association, marked a new level in relations between the community and the mosque, which has been the object of curiosity and some controversy since it opened in Westbury in 1984.

"What we hope is that having an event like this will lead to a greater understanding, both for our neighbors in regards to Islam, and for us in regards to the needs of the community," said Dr. Faroque Khan, spokesperson for the Islamic Center. "People don't want to just barge into a house of worship, so this is a way to invite them in to satisfy their curiosity."

Among the activities for visitors were continual showings of the movie "The Gift of Islam," art exhibits, a sampling of exotic foods, tours of the mosque, and a health fair geared to the needs of the community.

"Instead of focussing on religion, we want to focus on humankind," said Dr. Jamil Khan, a mosque member who is affiliated with New York University Hospital.

Standing behind a table of leaflets on pediatric care, she added that the mosque has many doctors and medical professionals as members, and that they would only be too happy to share their know-how with the community.

Other tables were filled with information on everything from prenatal and dental care to the latest news on childhood immunizations and sickle cell anemia.

"If the reception is positive, we'd like to repeat it on a regular basis," Dr. Faroque Khan said.

During his formal opening remarks, Khan said members of the Islamic Center had gained a better understanding of the issues facing the community over the past nine years, and wish to play a "pro-active" role in them. "Our objective is very simple," he explained, "to make this area a better place to live in."

Both Alphonse Campbell, who represented Mayor Ernest J. Strada and the Westbury Village Board of Trustees at the event, and Ron Smith, who attended on behalf of County Executive Thomas Gulotta, lauded the mosque as a positive addition to the community as a whole. Campbell said that "Westbury is a diverse community that prides itself on that diversity."

The center became the object of controversy beginning in 1988 when construction began on the mosque building itself, a large, arabesque structure which draws worshipers not only from the Westbury area, but from Roslyn, Manhasset and New Hyde Park as well (smaller numbers of worshipers come from as far away as Huntington and Brooklyn).

Used for religious services since shortly after building began, a number of residents have complained of parking problems and traffic congestion on local streets. To demonstrate a spirit of cooperation, the Center last month celebrated Eid Ul-Adha, one of the religion's major holidays, commemorating Abraham's offer to sacrifice his son, *at Bethpage State Park instead of at the mosque. The event drew close to six thousand people.*

During the open house the mosque had youths outside directing visitors to specified parking areas and to the homes of neighboring residents who had volunteered the use of their driveways for the day.

Since construction was completed on the mosque in late March, the center has begun making the facilities available for use by community organizations.

Khan said he believes there are currently about 10,000 Muslims on Long Island, served by seven mosques, in Roosevelt, Wyandanch, Valley Stream, Bay Shore, Selden and Westbury. The oldest mosque in North America, located in Ross, North Dakota, was established in 1929.

While the open house on June 5, 1993 was a good beginning, we had to work constantly in winning over the confidence and the "hearts" of our non-Muslim neighbors. We developed a methodology to accomplish this goal:

EDUCATION IN THE WESTBURY SCHOOL DISTRICT

We invited the Superintendent of Westbury Schools, Dr. Robert Pinckney, to address the ICLI members. Dr. Pinckney, after giving an overview of the school's programs and plans, suggested that one of the sorely needed areas in Westbury School District was the availability of work apprenticeships for students. Many of the members of ICLI are professionals, and we decided to follow-up on Dr. Pinckney's request. (See under CWCA)

CENTRAL WESTBURY CIVIC ASSOCIATION (CWCA)

We were invited to present ICLI's goals, etc. at one of the CWCA meetings. This was an opportunity to meet several active members of the community. During one of these meetings Dr. Robert Pinckney again emphasized the need for mentors for the students in WSD. This seemed like a perfect opportunity to initiate a joint program for high school students involving the WSD, CWCA and members of ICLI. This was the beginning of the medical apprenticeship program described below in a *Newsday* article.

GOALS AND OBJECTIVES

Nassau County Medical Center is a 615-bed public hospital (the only one on Long Island) established over 60 years back. The basic mission of this hospital is to take care of patients, irrespective of race, color, religion, sex, disability, or source of payment.

In addition, NCMC has been at the forefront of education of physicians, nurses, therapists, dentists and students from many other disciplines. In response to the national need for increased participation by underrepresented groups in health care (women, Afro-Americans, Hispanics, etc.), and after discussion with community leaders - especially Central Westbury Civic Association - ICLI, the Department of Medicine at NCMC, and Westbury High School have initiated a pilot program for interested Westbury High School seniors who will participate in the school and hospital apprenticeship program, with an expected start date of September, 1996.

The objectives are to expose the students to issues of health care and methods of delivery of care, with the expectation that they in turn will be stimulated, interested, and hopefully pursue careers in health care and thereby fill a void. The NCMC staff in turn will get a better appreciation of the health needs of the students, their families, etc. We are excited about this project and feel it is a "win-win" situation.

The program was supervised by Dr. Tanveer Mir, an active member of ICLI and Associate Program Director in the Department of Medicine at NCMC. Mr. Daniel J. McCue, in his article in the *Westbury Times* on April 18, 1996, captured the essence of this program. Below, we reproduce the article in full.

Hospital Reaches Out to Local Students
By Daniel J. McCue
The Westbury Times, April 18, 1996

It started with a casual conversation after a local civic association meeting.

Now, as a result of it, the Nassau County Medical Center and Westbury High School are teaming up to create a work apprenticeship program for students interested in science and medicine.

"This originated, basically, with a Central Westbury Civic Association meeting," explained Dr. Faroque A. Khan, Chairman of the Department of Medicine at the medical center. "Superintendent Dr. Robert D. Pinckney was giving a presentation about the schools, and afterwards I said, "Is there anything we can help with?"

Dr. Pinckney's answer was, "Yes."

One of the critical problems for students in Westbury was a lack of readily available role models in the professional fields. Inspired by a successful partnership with a local bank, the superintendent told Dr. Khan he'd like to create mentoring programs with a wide range of professionals.

With that Dr. Khan, a member of the Islamic Center of Long Island in Westbury, went about the task of building a bridge between his doctors and staff and local school students.

"This is a public hospital and I believe we should serve the public in every way possible," Dr. Khan said. "We've had health fairs and the like in the past, but really becoming involved in educating the next generation of adults is something we haven't delved into until now. I'm hoping that this pilot program will become a well-rounded model for public health facilities across the state."

The program, which is expected to be formalized in time for the start of school next September, will be conducted under the auspices of NCMC's Department of Medicine.

In recent months, as the groundwork was being laid for the formal introduction of the program, there has been a regular flow of professionals and students between the two buildings.

"We've held, I think, three sessions at the high school itself," Dr. Khan said. "During the first, we conducted a seminar on the importance of preserving one's health. At another, we had speakers talk about the impact of personal habits on one's overall well-being, and in May, we plan to have another session, this one focusing on nutrition."

During black-history month in February, Dr. Khan brought a special visitor to the school, Dr. Bernard Harris, an astronaut and the first African-American to walk in space.

Then as a follow-up, earlier this month, seven tenth-grade students spent several hours at the hospital speaking with physicians from various disciplines and extensively touring the facility.

"They talked to all manner of professionals, from cardiologists to pediatricians and on down the line," Dr.

43

Khan said. "In fact, at the end of their visit, they really didn't want to leave."

Newsday, in its September 10, 1996 issue also described the program in detail. Below, we reproduce some portions of this article which was titled *For 6 Students, Apprenticeship is "Nassau Hope."*

For 6 Students, Apprenticeship is "Nassau Hope"
By Betty Ommerman
Newsday, **Sunday, September 10, 1996**

Six Westbury High School seniors are discovering first hand what it's like to be part of a large hospital's medical staff. The students, three young men and three young women, are part of the pilot Medical Apprenticeship Program at Nassau County Medical Center, East Meadow.

The program, a cooperative venture between the high school and the hospital's Department of Medicine, began last month in response to the national need for increased participation in health care by underrepresented groups. Since the school, in Old Westbury, has an interracial student body, it was decided at a Westbury Central Civic Association meeting last year to help implement the program. Dr. Faroque Khan, chairman of the medical center's Department of Medicine, Westbury Superintendent Robert D. Pinckney and John Iannucci, coordinator of the high school's Medical Apprenticeship Program, worked out the details.

"Many young people have an interest in the medical field and the potential to succeed," Iannucci said. "The students chosen are in the upper half of the class academically and have the potential for making it through vigorous training."

Students take their academic studies in the morning, beginning at 7:30 a.m., then are bused to the hospital in the afternoon, where they stay from 12:30 to 3 p.m.

After an orientation period, the students were assigned to various medical departments where they're working under the supervision of medical staffers. The areas include ambulatory clinics, cardiology testing, geriatrics, physical rehabilitation and research.

Andrew Smellie, one of the seniors, is learning about cholesterol and diabetes while helping take blood pressure and pulse readings at one of the clinics. "I always knew I would enter the medical field," he said. "I'm just trying to find out which specific area I want. Right now, I'm focusing on the general primary care of patients and beginning a project where I'm surveying patients' medical and attendance compliance."

Elisa de los Santos, in cardiology, and Keesha Mullen, in geriatrics, hope to become obstetricians. "I do echo cardiograms and study cardiograms of patients in intensive care," Elisa said. Keesha gets to observe tube feeding of some geriatric patients and is learning medical terminology. "I also try to make patients feel comfortable."

Anamika Dey, who assists with sodium chloride emissions in DNA research, says she decided two years ago she wanted to be either a medical researcher or a physician.

"I like working side by side with researchers and learning from them," she said.

Other participating students are Vladimir Leonard, physical rehabilitation, and Justin Palmer, clinic.

"Students are expected to keep a journal of their experiences. They will also give a talk at a hospital assembly as the school year progresses," Khan said. Additionally, students will be given a project and have to report back to their mentors. "A graduation ceremony will be held in April or May, at which time they will present their work," Khan said.

The students received regular evaluations and were invited to the annual dinner of the graduating doctors from the Department of Medicine, where the student representative made a presentation on behalf of the student apprentices. Several of the students, after graduation from Westbury High School, pursued careers in health fields. The community of Westbury/New Cassel appreciated the efforts ICLI made in improving the educational standards, and awarded the *Community Education Award* to Dr. Faroque Khan for "Program of dedication, outreach and opportunities to the students of Westbury" on May 1, 1997.

This program was also described in the newsletter of the Westbury School District, with comments by the graduates of the program. In the February 1999 newsletter, one of the graduates, Magda Pierre, wrote:

Magda Pierre is a Westbury High School graduate currently in her first year at Nassau Community College. Magda was enrolled in the School-to-Career program at Westbury High School, performing an apprenticeship at Nassau County Medical Center. Magda recently visited the high school to speak with John Iannucci, Westbury's School Business Partnerships Coordinator, to thank him for helping her to gain valuable experience toward pursuing her career goal as a general practice physician.

"I am very fortunate to have been part of the program because I was doing what first-year medical students were doing," said Magda. "Now I have a clear understanding of what the medical field is like and what I have to do to contribute."

While apprenticing at Nassau County Medical Center, Magda was exposed to the ER, radiology department, research lab, physical therapy department, surgery, ICU, the MRI and CAT Scan machines and many other areas of the hospital.

"Going into college, I felt confident, and it stems from my learning experiences, both at the medical center and Westbury High School," added Magda. "The teachers of Westbury High School and the staff at the Nassau County Medical Center are some of the people who have left a distinct positive imprint on my life. They have really made a big difference."

OTHER INITIATIVES
Blood Drive:

The Islamic Center of Long Island, in collaboration with the New York Blood Bank, arranged for a blood donation drive, held at the center. In addition to members of ICLI, many of the neighbors joined in this project; thereby, they had a chance to visit and tour ICLI and meet with members.

New Cassel Environmental Project:

In the immediate vicinity of ICLI, there is the town of New Cassel that has an area which is believed to be contaminated and environmentally unsafe. Several members of ICLI joined in demonstrations, writing petitions, calling politicians urging them to rectify this environmental hazard.

School-Board Elections:

ICLI made its premises available for the school-board candidates to present their viewpoints. Most of the contestants made it a point to meet and share their views with ICLI members.

Public Health Clinic:

About half a mile from ICLI, a Department of Health Primary Care Clinic has been in operation. Several members of ICLI took an active role in the affairs of this clinic, and two got elected to the Advisory Board of this clinic.

Lawn of the Month:

I recall in the early years of ICLI's presence, some neighbors stated, "This mosque will bring down our home property values." Now the situation is reversed, and our efforts in improving the education standards are being appreciated. Brother Habeeb Ahmad deserves special commendation for his volunteer efforts in maintaining the landscaping of ICLI. This has been recognized by the Central Westbury Civic Association with the award of the *Lawn of the Month* for the past several years.

Holiday Greetings:

In 1999 the month of *Ramadhan* was celebrated and observed by Muslims during December which is also the time for Christmas. ICLI management sent the following message, along with a box of cookies to the immediate neighbors of ICLI (about 110 families). This message conveyed the Islamic concept of the birth of the Prophet Jesus.

Mary and Jesus
(Peace be Upon Them)

In the Quran (God's final message to humanity):

In the Name of Allah (God), The Merciful, The Compassionate.

AND LO! The angels said: "O Maryam (Mary)! Behold, God has elected thee and made thee pure, and raised thee above all the women of the world. Q3:42 O Maryam (Mary)! Behold, God sends thee the glad tidings, through a word from Him, (of a son) who shall become known as the Christ Jesus, son of Maryam (Mary), of great honor in this world and in the Hereafter. And he shall speak unto men in his cradle, and a grown man, and shall be of the righteous. Q3:45-46
Whereupon the child spoke out, "Behold, I am a servant of God. He has vouchsafed unto me revelation and made me a Prophet, and made me blessed wherever I may be, and He has enjoined upon me prayer and charity as long as

47

I live. He made me dutiful to my mother and has not made me haughty or
bereft of grace. Hence, peace was upon me on the day when I was born, and
(will be upon me) on the day of my death, and on the day when I shall be
raised to life (again)! Q19:30-33
Jesus (peace be upon him) said:
"Verily God is my sustainer as well as your sustainer, so worship Him (alone);
this is a straight way. Q3:50-51
God is just and right in whatever he says.

This gesture was greatly appreciated by the neighbors, and we received many thank-you's. One neighbor brought in a turkey, and Joseph Jolly wrote: *Thank you for the cookies. It's been a pleasure having you as a neighbor in Westbury. All good things for you and your congregation in the New Year.*

I have spent considerable time in describing the community initiatives of ICLI, since I believe that it's only with such programs and projects that Muslims will be able to overcome the stereotypes and myths being perpetrated. On Long Island we have made significant progress in overcoming these stereotypes. However, we continue to receive reports of unfortunate events resulting from prejudices and misinformation. The most recent glaring example was highlighted in the November 1999 issue of *The Minaret*. The lead article was:

Bias Against an Islamic School
The applications for building a branch of New Horizon School in Orange County, California, was rejected on technical grounds. The undercurrent that led to the blocking of such a non-controversial project is very disturbing. The November issue of "Minaret" published a detailed report on the project and the opposition and support it is receiving from the people.

The work done at ICLI to win the hearts and minds of its neighbors was best summarized in an editorial in *The Westbury Times* in November 1998, which we reproduce in its entirety.

Islamic Center Truly Part of Our Community
By Daniel J. McCue
The Westbury Times

Perhaps it was all just a matter of having to overcome a bit of unfortunate timing.

Several years ago, when members of what would become the Islamic Center of Long Island first began to meet on a property fronted by Brush Hollow Road in

Westbury, many of their neighbors expressed grave concerns about the new arrivals.

It wasn't just that another church had bought property in the area - a perennial gripe among taxpaying homeowners aggrieved at seeing another chunk of precious land disappear from the tax roles.

No, it was fear, mainly, that drove a wedge between neighbors. Though a few Muslims had always lived among us, the timing of the construction of the Westbury Mosque could, perhaps, not have been more inopportune: news reports, day in and day out, filled local living rooms with images of what was described as "Islamic Fundamentalism" and "Islamic terrorism."

To make matters worse for the young, but growing, Islamic Center congregation, the Cold War was ending, and both the media and the movie industry felt the need to cast about and find a new villain. As often happens, the least understood among us, in this case Muslims, became the scapegoats.

For every "terrorist" gunned down by Stallone, and the like, in a Hollywood picture, another wary glance is cast at the Center in Westbury.

"Even people who have known us personally, for years, sometimes don't understand us," Dr. Qamar Zaman said the other night.

He then added a simple, but profound statement, "If I'm not an ambassador for Islam, who will be?"

Over the past several years, particularly the past five, the Islamic Center of Long Island has gone from being a widely misunderstood institution to a cornerstone, not just of Westbury, but of all Nassau County.

If the efforts of the Center's members began and ended with reaching out to the public to educate them about Islam, that would have been a truly significant undertaking.

However, the members of the Center, many of them doctors, accountants and educators, were not content to stop there.

First, they began offering weekend programs, providing medical and other expertise to the poor in the

Westbury and New Cassel areas; then, they became intimately involved with efforts such as those undertaken by the New Cassel Environmental Justice project; then too, in short order, ICLI members began to roll up their sleeves in an attempt to make a real difference in the local school district.

Speaking of the all-too-often-used stereotype of the "Islamic terrorist," Dr. Murad Hoffmann pointed out the other night that "no religion is responsible for what people will do with it."

The problem, from where we stand, is that when something is controversial, it gets full airing, but when people take what they stand for and do good with it, nary a grain of sand is moved in an effort to tell that tale.

With so much media out there today, with so many channels available on local cable alone, you'd think that media would do a better job at educating the public about the subtext and context of the stories it conveys. Sadly, we must admit they don't.

For instance, when the word "Palestinian" is used on television, most Americans think of "Muslims." In point of fact, many Palestinians are Christians.

When Saddam Hussein is shown on television, many Americans might presume - solely on the basis of his being in the Middle East - that he's a Muslim. Again, in point of fact, he is not. He is the leader of the Baath Party, an atheistic and fascist political entity.

More to the point, most Muslims don't even hail from the Middle East, instead tracing their roots back to places like India and Pakistan, Bosnia, and right here in the U.S.A.

Here in America, much is still misunderstood about the Islamic culture. In many respects, it is still a "foreign" philosophy to most Judeo-Christian citizens.

What is undeniable, though, is this: without the Islamic Center of Long Island and its members, our town and our county would be much-diminished places.

Chapter 6

AMERICAN MUSLIMS AND JEWS IN DIALOGUE (AMJID)

Quran 7:159
Of the people of Moses
There is a section
Who guide and do justice
In the light of truth.

As a child growing up in Kashmir, I had often heard my dad, Ghulam Hassan Khan, talk about his experiences when he was an Engineering student at Harvard University in Boston, MA, from 1928-1932. He often mentioned the kindness and affection his landlady (who was Jewish) showed towards him. The following are excerpts from his memoirs.

Some Reminiscences

After spending one year at 10 Trowbridge Street (1927-1928), I lodged for the second year (1928-1929) with a Jewish family. Mrs. Helen Drapen was the landlady. Besides my curiosity for knowing what the Jews were like, I preferred a Jewish home for dietary reasons. Like Muslims, they (i) did not eat pork, (ii) slaughtered the animals as we do. I had quite a few fellow students at my college who were Jews, and I was very friendly with them. Ganick and Ginnsberg were also Tau Bets. A nickname for Ginnsberg was "The Greasy Grind" - so hardworking he was. Mathew Gordon was another student friend, my size; he was called Tiny Nathan. He was a true type of his tribe - business mind-ed. I had a lovely time and fully enjoyed my stay at their home. They looked after me so well. A Jewish boy friend invited me to a swim at a beach in Boston. I stepped on a broken bottle, injured my foot badly. The foot was stitched at a local hospital and I remained on crutches for over 10 days. Luckily this happened during the summer vacation of 1929. Miss Rebecca (Beatrice) Drapen, the eldest daughter of the landlady, dressed my foot every day with loving care as if I was her real brother. They won my heart. Among themselves they were considerate, affectionate and very helpful.

At home the young lady was known by the Jewish name Rebecca. At school she was enrolled as Beatrice. At home they read Yeddish newspapers and spoke Yeddish as well as English.

My first contact with members of the Jewish faith happened after I migrated to the United States from Kashmir, during my residency training in 1966 in Barberton, Ohio. A year later, my wife Arfa and I came to New York to further pursue our medical training. We started at Queens Hospital Center, which was managed by Long Island Jewish Medical Center. From 1967 we had daily contact with Jewish colleagues, several of whom played a major role as advisors and helped us in the transition and cultural adjustment. For me, personally, the role Drs. Nathan Seriff and Edward Meilman played in my professional advancement was crucial. Both my wife Arfa and I were given important management responsibilities. In fact, 33 years later Arfa still works at LIJMC. I moved on in 1987. While we had daily contact with our Jewish colleagues, we never had a chance to engage in a serious, meaningful interfaith dialogue. All this changed in January 1992, when ICLI received a call from Ms. Bobby Rosenzweig from Temple Beth El, a prominent Reform synagogue in Great Neck, New York. Mrs. Rosenzweig had inquired about Muslims in Long Island who might be interested in having a meeting with Rabbi Jerome Davidson and Ms. Rosenzweig. We accepted this invitation. Al Haaj Ghazi Khankan and I visited Temple Beth El, and met with Rabbi Davidson and Ms. Rosenzweig. This was the initiation of our very successful interaction with members of Temple Beth El. Being that this was a unique and new experience for us, we had to develop an agenda and method of operation with a focus on topics of mutual interest.

I was guided in this interaction by the following *Quranic* chapters:

> *Chapter 29, Verse 46*
> *And dispute ye not*
> *With the People of the Book,*
> *Except with means better*
> *(Than mere disputation), unless*
> *It be with those of them*
> *Who inflict wrong (and injury);*
> *But say, "We believe*
> *In the Revelation which has*
> *Come down to us and in that*
> *Which came down to you;*
> *Our God and your God*

Is One; and it is to Him
We bow (in Islam)."

Mere disputations are futile. In order to achieve our purpose as true standard-bearers for Allah, we shall have to find true common grounds of belief, as stated in the latter part of this verse, and also to show by our urbanity, kindness, sincerity, truth, and genuine anxiety, for the good of others, that we are not cranks or merely seeking selfish or questionable aims.

Chapter 16, Verse 125
*Invite (all) to the Way
Of thy Lord with wisdom
And beautiful preaching;
And argue with them
In ways that are best
And most gracious:
For thy Lord knoweth best,
Who have strayed from His Path,
And who receive guidance.*

In this wonderful passage are laid down principles of religious teaching, which are good for all time. But where are the Teachers with such qualifications? We must invite all to the Way of Allah, and expound His Universal Will; we must do it with wisdom and discretion, meeting people on their own ground and convincing them with illustrations from their own knowledge and experience, which may be very narrow, or very wide. Our preaching must be, not dogmatic, not self-regarding, not offensive, but gentle, considerate, and such as would attract their attention. Our manner and our arguments should not be acrimonious, but modelled on the most courteous and the most gracious example, so that the hearer may say to himself, " This man is not dealing merely with dialectics; he is not trying to get a rise out of me; he is sincerely expounding the faith that is in him, and his motive is the love of man and the love of Allah."

In my opinion, in order to have a successful interfaith dialogue the following are some areas which should be given serious consideration -

Attitude

One needs to approach the dialogue with a sense of humility, an open mind, and be willing to listen patiently to the other viewpoint.

Respect and Hospitality

It is important to show respect to the partners in dialogue. Hospitality in one's home can be a big "ice breaker." We found the ingredients found in a "Samoosa" or "Barfi" can initiate a healthy dialogue regarding foods.

Define Positions Clearly

It is important to clearly explain, early on in the dialogue, the role of the Quran and Sunnah in a Muslim's life. This dialogue represents a good opportunity to present Islam as a way of life. When prayer time arrives, excuse yourselves and pray. "Faith in action."

Compare Similar Items

Often faith and culture get mixed up. A recent example was the wide publicity which was given to female circumcision in Africa. We had one of our members from Africa explain this entire topic, and the group quickly realized that this was a local African custom which had nothing to do with Islam or being a Muslim.

Keep a Balance in Participants

We chose approximately 12 members in each group, with representation by both women and men. The group needs to have compatibilities with each other.

Establish Ground Rules, Agenda and Parameters

We decided to focus, initially, on non-political and non-confrontational items. We stressed the commonality of the religions and agreed to disagree when discussions of topics like Jerusalem warranted a difference of opinion.

With these guidelines in hand, we followed a set agenda, alternating sites and speakers, and the following is a list of topics which have been discussed in the first three years.

American Muslims and Jews in Dialogue (AMJID)

The Quran, Sunnah and Hadith	April 14, 1992
The Jewish Scriptures	June 2, 1992

<u>Results in Dialogue</u>

We believe the dialogue between ICLI and Temple Beth El representatives has been mutually beneficial. Briefly summarizing the results of this dialogue:

Positive Image of Islam and Muslims on Long Island

Very favorable reports regarding ICLI have been published in *Newsday, The New York Times, The Westbury Times* and *Jewish World*. These articles have resulted in very favorable comments and response from readers of these articles. Interestingly, two of these articles in *The New York Times* and *Jewish World* were authored by Walter Ruby, who attended one of the dialogue sessions. A few examples will highlight this:

1. "LI Mosque is a Sign of Islam's Community Growth." *The New York Times*, February 25, 1993.
2. "Mosque Opens Doors to Neighbors." *Newsday*, June 6, 1993.
3. "Mosque Feted with Open House." *Westbury Times*, June 17, 1993.
4. "Long Island Jewish-Muslim Dialogue Group Works to Breakdown Stereotypes and Build the Bonds of Understanding." *Long Island Jewish World*, September 10-16, 1993.

5. Long Island Muslims and Jews Together in Worship." *Newsday*, November 13, 1993.
6. "In Tense Times, A Seder Stresses Unity." *Newsday*, March 23, 1994.
7. "Muslim Leaders on LI Temper Rhetoric and Focus on Local Social Problems." *The New York Times*, Sunday, May 1, 1994.

Television

Three separate TV shows were devoted to the activities of ICLI, and all three resulted from the dialogue. One was the Catholic channel's "God Squad," which was aired several times, nationally; the second one dealt with "Current Events on Long Island," and the third one was aired nationally on "MacNeil/Lehrer Newshour" in September 1993.

Student Exchange

One of the dialogue participants works in the Herricks' School District in Nassau County. Through her initiative, an ICLI representative gave an in-depth presentation to ALL the teachers of the Herricks' School District regarding Islam and Muslims, and after that over 200 senior students have visited ICLI and received firsthand information regarding Islam during June 1994.

Invited Lectures

The interfaith dialogue has had a ripple effect in other communities in Nassau County. As an example, Mr. Ghazi Khankan, Director of Communications and Interfaith Dialogue at ICLI, made numerous presentations, given interviews to news and TV reporters, and represented ICLI at various interfaith dialogues since September 1993. Also, Mr. Ghazi Khankan was invited to give a workshop regarding AMJID at the Sixty-Second Annual National Hebrew Congregation held in San Francisco in October 1993, and attended by over 6,000 Reformed Jews.

In summary, the experience of AMJID has been extremely beneficial. We have developed a better understanding of each other. Stereotypes have gradually been replaced by realistic image, and the Muslims of Nassau County have received favorable write-ups in local, regional and national press and TV.

Talking of stereotypes, a very prevalent perception regarding Muslims follows:

May 4, 1993, *New York Times* - Ari Goldman quotes:
Muslims are individuals with long beards and turbans who run around on camels with swords in their hand and have two harems with four wives in each. They are fanatical, ignorant and illiterate people.

Personally, I have yet to meet a Muslim who fits this widely perceived description. During one of our discussions focused on stereotypes, one member from Temple Beth El, after a long pause, remarked, "But you are normal people." I guess she was trying to reconcile the common perception regarding Muslims with the reality of meeting Muslims who were concerned with family, faith, education, environment, and health. As the years went by, we developed friendships and a level of comfort, and at times of crisis heard from each other. Just to cite several examples:

World Trade Center Bombing
After this unfortunate and tragic terrorist act, there was mass hysteria and Muslims were given very negative publicity. At this time it was comforting to receive a call from Mrs. Bobby Rosenzweig. She expressed the support of Temple Beth El.

Bosnia Genocide
Steve Limmer drafted a strong appeal to President Bush, Clinton and others about the "ethnic cleansing" being perpetrated in Bosnia.

Hebron Massacre
On Friday, February 25, 1994 - 14 *Ramadhan* 1414, 50 Muslim worshippers in prayer were killed, and an additional 150 were wounded. This senseless terrorist attack by Dr. Baruch Goldstein caused an immense outrage in the Muslim community, and I shared with ICLI members the sentiments expressed by AMJID participants.

<u>Rabbi Jerome Davidson</u> *We are outraged by this violation of basic human values. We urge Israel to take stronger steps to control violence by Israelis against innocent Arabs and Muslims.*

<u>Ms. Bobby Rosenzweig</u> *About 70 members of the temple prayed. We are angry, ashamed and disgusted. Please convey this sense of grief to all members.*

While the AMJID participants met and talked about various issues, several events were arranged at Temple Beth El and ICLI, where the entire community was invited. The following are some examples:

November 12, 1993
Temple Beth El: *Towards Greater Understanding and Cooperation Between Muslims and Jews in America* by Professor Sulayman S. Nyang, Howard University, Washington.

November 6, 1994
ICLI: *Prophet Moses in the Torah and Quran.* Keynote Address: *Muslims and Jews in America. What Unites Us?* by Rabbi Jerome Davidson.

November 22, 1997
Temple Beth El: Presentation during *Havdalah* hour by Drs. Arfa and Faroque Khan on *Hajj.*

March 1, 1998
Temple Beth El: *What an American Jew Should Know About the People and Religion of Islam.* Three perspectives, followed by a presentation by Sayyid Mohd Sayeed, Secretary General of the Islamic Society of North America, on *Challenges Facing Muslims in North America.*

June 7, 1998
ICLI: *What It Means To Be A Jew In America. The Way It Was and The Way It Is. How Did We Get There?* A perspective of three generations.

December 5, 1999

ICLI: One City : Three Faiths - The Meaning of Jerusalem in Judaism, Christianity and Islam. Rabbi Karen Bender, Msgr. Thomas Hartman, Habeeb Ahmed.

Since 1992 when we initiated this dialogue, we have come a long, long way. We have learned from each other. We have developed better appreciation of each other's viewpoint, and we have been able to put a face on the Muslim community in Long Island.

The session held on June 7, 1998 is a good example of this. The topic *What It Means To Be A Jew In America* was suggested by us, primarily to learn how the Jewish community in North America has been able to accomplish so much in such a short period of time. We heard this perspective from three generations - Dr. Isidore Bernstein described his experience in the 40's and 50's, when he had to struggle against prejudices against Jews who were denied admission to universities and other public areas. Dr. Martin Hoffert gave his experience in the early 50's and 60's, when he was able to do a lot more than Dr. Bernstein, and many more centers of higher education had started accepting qualified Jewish students. The final presentation was by Mrs. Stephanie Propos Fishkin, part-time attorney, mother, volunteer. She described her upbringing and education in the 70's and 80's, wherein she felt free to choose her college, career and combine her personal and professional lives.

This event was very educational for the Muslims, since many of them are facing the stereotypes and prejudices which the Jews faced earlier. The message was clear. If you commit your human fiscal and intellectual resources in an organized manner, the obstacles and prejudices can be overcome.

The AMJID group has now reached a level of maturity where we can bring up topics where we know there are major differences of opinion. During the session on Jerusalem in December 1999, we got a much better appreciation of the viewpoints of other faiths regarding the significance of Jerusalem to Jews, Christians and Muslims. One Jewish member commented after the session, *We have to unlearn lots of things we learned about Muslims.*

In March 2000 we held another session focused on the political implication of Jerusalem for Muslims, Christians and Jews. At Temple Beth El, several hundred attendees, most of whom were Jewish, heard, many for the first time, the Palestinian perspective of this issue. They received a firsthand report of the ground realities - house demolitions, limited access for Palestinians, ongoing land confiscation, and restriction of building permits from Khalid Turrani, Executive Director of American Muslims for Jerusalem. Such a frank discussion would have been unthinkable, particularly in a synagogue, before the AMJID dialogue was started.

This pretty much summarizes the goals, objective and accomplishments of the interfaith dialogue.

Chapter 7

THE SIGNIFICANCE OF GETTING A TRAFFIC LIGHT AT ICLI ENTRANCE?

MUSLIMS AND THE POLITICAL PROCESS: *THINK GLOBAL AND ACT LOCAL.*

The Council of American Islamic Relations (CAIR), a Washington-based Islamic advocacy group, conducted a poll of 878 Muslims in December 1999. An overwhelming 96 percent of the respondents stated that Muslims should get involved in local and national politics.

While the sentiments expressed are very encouraging, it has been our experience at ICLI that many Muslims, particularly immigrants, are not very familiar with the system of government, the manner in which the two-party system operates, the role and importance of local committees, the process of becoming delegates, etc., etc. Partly to address and rectify this deficiency, and also to educate and engage the various leaders/candidates in issues of importance to Muslims, ICLI, over a period of years, invited and welcomed local, state, and national candidates to meet with the community. The following examples highlight the manner in which ICLI was able to meet its objectives and, in the process, introduce key political leaders to Al Islam and its followers, the Muslims.

GUBERNATORIAL ELECTION

In 1994, ICLI extended an invitation to both candidates, Governor Mario Cuomo and the challenger, State Senator George Pataki. Senator Pataki accepted the invitation and visited ICLI on August 14, 1994. The polls at that stage had him trailing Governor Cuomo by 24 points. This event was the first official public meeting of Senator Pataki on Long Island, and the Muslim community was particularly proud to have this honor. Subsequent events are well known. Senator Pataki beat Governor Cuomo and is now in his second term as Governor of New York. Based on his visit to ICLI and his positive interaction with the Muslims, he was endorsed by key members of ICLI, some of whom took out advertisements in support of him in newspapers widely circulated in the

Muslim community. Some excerpts of Mr. Pataki's visit to ICLI are reproduced below from the August 18, 1994 issue of the *Westbury Times*.

Campaign Trail Leads to Westbury
George Pataki Visits Islamic Center
By Danny McCue
Westbury Times, August 18, 1994

State Senator George Pataki, the conservative Republican candidate who has proven to be Governor Mario Cuomo's stiffest competition since the election of 1982, brought his gubernatorial campaign to Westbury Sunday morning, visiting the Islamic Center of Long Island on Brush Hollow Road.

The stop, one of several Mr. Pataki made throughout Long Island over the weekend also marked the first time the candidate had interacted with a significant number of Muslim voters.

In his welcoming remarks, Faroque A. Khan of the Islamic Center spoke of the prejudicial image with which Muslims are often portrayed by the media. "We are seen as fanatic and ignorant people," he said, contrasting that image with the extremely important and significant contributions Muslims have made to society in the areas of mathematics, language and sciences.

Mr. Khan also inspired much laughter when he talked of Muslim voting habits. "Muslims in America are 33 percent Democrat, 32 percent Republican and 33 percent Independent, he said. "So you see, Senator, there's a lot of room to work here."

Acknowledging Mr. Khan's comment about voter registration in the Muslim community, Mr. Pataki said, "This election is not so much about replacing a Democrat with a Republican or replacing Cuomo with Pataki, it's fully about changing the direction of the state. We simply cannot afford four more years of a failed criminal justice system. We need change and this election is about change."

Before the brief tour of the mosque which culminated his visit, Mr. Pataki vowed to remain aware of the sensitivities of the Muslim community.

"Whenever a community is singled out unfairly for discriminatory treatment, whether it's from the gov-

ernment, the private sector, local government, or the press, it is the obligation of the governor of the state to stand up and speak."

HISTORIC VISIT BY NASSAU LEGISLATURE TO ISLAMIC CENTER OF LONG ISLAND ON JANUARY 10, 1996.

Nassau County, a suburb of New York City with a population of over 1 million, went through a major governmental reorganization. Following a suit brought by minority members, a judge ruled that a new legislative form of government needs to be formed to give better representation to all segments of the population.

In November 1995 an election for this newly created 19-member legislative body was held. The Muslim community played an active role, both during and after the election. Several legislative candidates visited the Islamic Center of Long Island and met with members of the Muslim community. The 19-member legislative body took the oath of office on January 1, 1996.

Muslims of Nassau County, representing approximately 20,000, hosted a reception on Wednesday, January 10, 1996 at ICLI. A cross-section of the Muslim leadership of Nassau County met with the 14 legislators (some with spouses), who spent over four hours at ICLI. This reception received wide coverage in the local press and the program consisted of:

a) Excerpts from the highly acclaimed documentary, *Islam in America*, produced by *The Christian Science Monitor* were shown.

b) Legislators were given an overview of the contributions Muslims are making in the areas of:
    i.   health delivery
    ii. crime prevention
    iii. environmental control
    iv. educational improvement

An example from each of these topics was shared with the legislators, with a focus on the local scene.

c) Each of the 14 legislators present addressed the gathering and expressed thanks and gratitude, and marveled at the initiative shown by the Muslims in inviting the entire legislative body to the Islamic Center.

d) The function was completed with a fine home-cooked Afghan dinner and, during this session, the legislators met and discussed issues of mutual concern with representatives from their own legislative districts.

Following this highly successful event, a number of news articles were published regarding the event. A few excerpts follow.

Newsday - **January 12, 1996**
Heading: *Island Muslims Find Their Voice* -
plus a picture of 14 legislators observing the Muslims in prayer.

Westbury Times - **January 18, 1996**
Heading on Front Page: *Legislators Receive Education in Islam* -
two-page main feature article with five pictures of the leg-islators and Muslims. This paper is widely distributed in the area surrounding the Islamic Center of Long Island.

The New York Times - **Sunday, January 21, 1996**
Heading (Long Island Journal Section): *Afghan Gourmet* -
description of the event, with focus on women and Afghan food, and two pictures from the function.

Some relevant excerpts from the reception:

Bruce Blakeman - Presiding Officer of Legislature
We were invited to attend tonight by Dr. Khan, who offered to give us an overview of the Muslim community in Nassau. I think it's important to understand the issue of concern to every segment of our community. The high turnout tonight is a real indication of the legislators' interest and commit-ment to the public that elected us.

Ed Mangano - 17th District
I have very little knowledge of the Muslim community. For me, this is a learning experience.

Dennis Dunne - 15th District
Truly, this community is comprised of wonderful people; it's really an honor to be asked to come to their place of worship.

Richard Nicollello - 9th District
Tonight really made me realize how strong a component the Muslim community can be when it comes to social ills. I was particularly struck by the emphasis they put on the strong family unit.

64

Darlene Harris - 1st District
*This is beautiful. . . . . being invited to attend a function like this,
held by individuals of another faith, is extremely meaningful to me.*

In addition to the 14 legislators, Mr. Stephen J. Sabbeth, Chairman of the Nassau Democratic Party also attended and addressed the group.

Diane Ketcham of *The New York Times: An amazing phenomenon. Almost an entire legislative body ate dinner together.*

Based on this very positive experience, the Muslim community in Nassau County will be taking an even greater, more active role in the political process at all levels of government - town, village, legislative, congressional, senatorial and presidential.

Another distinguished guest of ICLI was New York State Comptroller H. Carl McCall, who is the highest-ranking elected Democrat in New York State. His visit was on May 31, 1998, and highlights are excerpted below.

> *As comptroller, Mr. McCall is the sole trustee of the 880,000-member State and Local Retirement System, and is responsible for investing a pension fund valued at over one hundred billion dollars.*
>
> *In his prepared remarks, Mr. McCall described his role as the Chief Fiscal Officer of New York State, and his experiences (some not so pleasant) as an African-American in this elected position. He emphasized the need for groups to get involved in the political process, and the importance of getting to know and holding politicians accountable and responsive, particularly at the local level.*
>
> *In a lively question-and-answer period with an over-flow crowd, Mr. McCall addressed questions ranging from public education and the mechanism for distribution of funds for education, his recent impressions from a visit to the Middle East, emphasizing the need for a balanced approach by the US government to issues in the Middle East, his overall plans for investment of pension funds – encouraging attendees to submit proposals for his review, etc., etc. Several non-Muslim members from the Westbury School District, including Superintendent of Schools, Chair of the Westbury School Board, etc. attended, and they were appreciative of the efforts of the Muslim community.*
>
> *When questioned about his future goals, Mr. McCall stated that he was seeking re-election as Comptroller of New*

York State for 1998, and might consider future election as Senator from New York in the year 2000 and/or Governor in 2002. The group was very impressed with Mr. McCall's presentation, honesty, and clarity, and wished him well in his re-election. This was the first meeting of the highest-ranked elected Democrat in New York State with the Muslim community. (P.S. Mr. McCall was re-elected comptroller in 1998 with the largest margin of votes ever recorded in this particular race.)

While these high-profile visits receive lots of news coverage, we need to emphasize the role of the staff in the various political parties. Mr. Gene Turner, Chief of Staff of Congressman Peter King of the Third District, visited ICLI many times and shared his experience regarding the "nuts and bolts" of setting up successful politically active and effective units.

Mr. Darren Block, Chief of Staff of the Nassau Democratic Legislative Party, along with the Executive Director Mr. Vincent Grasso, spent an entire morning at ICLI explaining the vision, structure of the Democratic Party in Nassau and invited involvement of the Muslims. The advice which these seasoned politicians have given us can be summarized as:

1. Integrate at local level. This is the key to success.
1. Identify issues at local, national and international levels and pursue them aggressively.
3. Find common ground and build on that.

CONGRESSMAN PETER KING

Congressman King represents the Third Congressional District in Long Island. He has been a frequent visitor to ICLI, understands and sympathizes with issues of concern to Muslims, and often seeks the opinion of the ICLI leadership regarding issues affecting Muslims.

EXECUTIVE THOMAS GULOTTA

Mr. Gulotta has also shown a keen interest and sensitivity towards Muslims, and Al Haaj Ghazi Khankan was appointed by the County Executive as a liaison to the Muslim community. Ghazi Khankan gets invited regularly to give invocations at important county functions.

While Muslims often get excited and emotionally involved with issues which rightly concern them - Palestine, Kashmir, Bosnia, Chechnya, Kosova, Sudan, Eritrea, etc., etc., I feel the energies and strategy for Muslims should be focused at the local level where they can make a real difference. Once that's done, the impact will eventually be felt at the national and international level, as well. We should work from the bottom up and minimize the top-down approach. An astute visitor to ICLI once remarked, after seeing the newly installed traffic light at the entrance to ICLI, *Looks like you guys have arrived politically*. He was, perhaps, referring to the importance the local county government attaches to the needs of ICLI and the expedient manner in which they responded when ICLI requested a traffic light at its entrance.

The lessons I learned dealing with politicians as spokesperson of ICLI have been:

> 1.   Most, if not all, are receptive, willing and at times even anxious to visit and meet Muslims and learn about Al Islam.
>
> 2.   The Muslim communities need to identify individuals who have the interest and skills to engage in a political discourse, and then those individuals - preferably men and women - should develop programs and plans to fulfill the set agenda.
>
> 3.   Muslims have a large voting block which can have an impact. This should be used effectively.
>
> 4.   While fundraisers are a part of the system, I feel if done as a group it has a much larger impact.

Six Muslims - three women and three men - recently participated in the celebration of the Democratic Party's victory in Nassau County. We chose to go under the banner of "ICLI." The result was we were given a separate VIP booth, and most of the political leaders made it a point to come and visit us in this booth. The impact of six individuals organized as a group was a lot more effective than six separate individuals would have had, amongst a crowd of over seven hundred.

In summary, the Muslims need to put on their "thinking hats" and participate in events in an organized manner. I have listed a few of the events hosted at ICLI. Over the years ICLI has hosted dozens of candidates and elected officials at ICLI. To give a brief synopsis of these visitors:

Congresswoman Carolyn McCarthy   District 4 New York State
Congressman Gary Ackerman   District 5 New York State

67

Senator Robert Toricelli	New Jersey
Senator Timothy Johnson	South Dakota
NYS Assemblyman Thomas DiNapoli	Chairman, Nassau County Democratic Party
New York State Senator	Michael Balboni
Morshed Alam	NYS Senate Candidate
Matthew Cuomo	Nassau Legislature Candidate
Donna Ferrara	NYS Assemblywoman

and many more. Our philosophy has been - *Come and present your view; hear from the Muslims, and then they will decide whom to support.*

Chapter 8

UNIQUE GEOGRAPHIC CHALLENGES FOR ICLI

Coping with Unexpected Challenges: Terrorism, Airline Crashes

The location of ICLI in Westbury, Long Island about 20 miles east of Manhattan - the media capital of the USA - brings some special challenges and opportunities. Over the past decade we have been engaged in, affected by, involved in handling the aftermath of natural and terrorists' activities. Four specific incidents come to mind - World Trade Center bombing(1993), Oklahoma City bombing (April 19,1995), TWA Flight 800 crash (July 17,1996), and Egypt Air Flight 990 crash (Oct 21,1999). These incidents have had a profound impact on our community, and handling these crises has been a learning experience for us, from which several lessons can be learned. This also brings to light the Quranic Surah 94 verses 5 and 6. *So, verily with every difficulty there is relief. Verily, with every difficulty there is relief.*

World Trade Center Bombing

On Friday Feb 26, 1993, while the Muslims were in a state of deep introspection, self analysis during the month of *Ramadhan*, we were shocked to hear the news of the World Trade Center (WTC) bombing resulting in the death of six and injuries to over a thousand. Living in Long Island in close proximity to the WTC, and having visited the WTC several times, this tragedy had a big impact on me. While the initial speculations were focussed on groups such as the Serbs, I was totally shocked when subsequent events and investigations would implicate and convict "Muslims." The WTC bombing resulted in the imprinting of Muslims with terrorism in the minds of Americans. The results were palpable, for example, when subsequent tragedies such as the Oklahoma bombing (1995) and the TWA Fl 800 crash (1996) occurred, the initial suspects were the Muslims. Terrorist actions carried out in the name of Islam and Muslims are, of course, totally un-Islamic. No religion condones the killings of civilians, and Islam specifically forbids suicide. *And do not*

69

kill yourselves (nor kill one another). Surely Allah is Most Merciful to you. (Quran 4:29) Tragically, the terrorist actions by Muslims get widespread and front-page coverage. Consider the following facts: According to the *US State Dept Report, 1996 Global Terrorism: Year in Review,* 296 acts of International terrorism occurred -

11	in Africa
11	in Asia
24	in Eurasia
121	in Europe
84	in Latin America
45	in Middle East
0	in North America.

Of these one fourth (74) were anti-US -

50	in Latin America
8	in Europe
3	in Middle East
2	in Africa
11	in Eurasia

In another study compiled by the Muslim Public Affair Council, in 1998 there were a total of 111 anti-US attacks, defined as attacks against US facilities and attacks in which US citizens suffered casualties. Of these 111 -

87	originated in Latin America
13	in Western Europe
5	in Middle East
3	in Eurasia
3	in Africa

Tragically, most Americans in my view are totally unaware of these facts and they associate most, if not all, acts of terrorism with Muslims which is factually not correct.

Oklahoma City Bombing

On April 19, 1995, the bombing of Oklahoma City's Murray Federal Building killed 169 people and injured hundreds more. Patriot follower, Timothy McVeigh, and Terry Nichols were subsequently arrested and tried for this heinous crime. I recall the first forty-eight hours after

70

this crime were a nightmare for the Muslim community in the USA. There was a dark cloud of suspicion over Muslims; this was fanned by some media experts who labeled the suspects as "Middle Eastern." There were numerous instances of harassment, intimidation, and even violence against individuals who "looked" like Muslims, and against mosques - some being vandalized. There were instances of pregnant Muslim women aborting prematurely. It was indeed a dark moment for Muslims in America. In retrospect, from this adversity Muslims learned several lessons, and I believe it served as a wake-up call for Muslims. Some of them finally decided it was time to "come out of the closet" and speak and identify themselves as Muslims. In short, it was about time that Muslims took charge of their destiny and spoke for themselves. It wasn't long before another tragedy would occur and present a challenge for Muslims, once again - TWA Flight 800.

TWA Flight 800: Muslims' Response

On the evening of Wednesday, July 17, 1996 I first heard the reports of a plane crash off East Moriches, Long Island, not far from where I live. Soon it became obvious that in the crash of TWA 800, en route to Paris from JFK with 230 passengers and crew, there would be no survivors and the possibility of a bomb, missile, or mechanical failure was being considered. I recalled the initial reaction following the Oklahoma City bombing in April 1995. I wondered and worried about the anticipated Muslim bashing from news and media experts. I was reassured to hear President Clinton's remarks when he advised the people not to rush to any judgement. On July 19th, after the Friday Khutba, we at the Islamic Center of Long Island issued a statement which basically conveyed a message of condolence for the friends and families of this tragedy. We also learned that amongst the 230 passengers and crew there were several Muslims. We urged the media to refrain from any prejudgments, and to heed President Clinton's call for objective reporting based on facts and not hearsay or preconceived opinions.

On Sunday, July 21st, around 11:30 a.m. I received a call from Br. Ibrahim Hooper of the Council of American Islamic Relations in Washington, informing me about a memorial service scheduled at JFK Airport at 4 p.m. He urged us, and I agreed, that a Muslim presence at the services was essential. Details and further information regarding the

71

services were difficult to obtain, and I decided to go to the airport to attend. I gave myself plenty of time and arrived at Hanger 208 about 3 p.m. My anxiety mounted as I saw the area filled with security personnel, press vehicles, cameras, and general hustle and bustle. Who did I represent? Did I have an official invitation, etc., etc?

I was able to enter the main building and, after requesting to see the organizers of this service, I was led to a private room where all the clergy and dignitaries were gathered. I was, frankly, overcome with the warm reception given to me when I introduced myself as a Muslim and spokesperson for the Islamic Center of Long Island, Westbury. Very quickly I was incorporated into the main program; seating was arranged on the dais, and some of the comments prior to the function were:

John Cardinal O'Connor, Archbishop of New York: *I am glad you are here.*

Rev. L.B. Stewart, Chaplain, JFK Airport: *Am I glad to see you.*

Rev. James Devine, Chaplain, JFK Airport: *Thanks for taking the time and being part of this.*

The ceremony, titled "Prayer Service of Healing and Peace for Families, Friends, Colleagues, and Loved Ones on TWA Flight 800," lasted about two hours, with prayers in English, French, Hebrew, and Arabic. Over 2,000 attendees were present. I particularly remember, during the remarks I made, a middle-aged lady in tears left a framed picture of a young individual on the dais.

After the formal remarks, I stood along with Mayor Rudolph Guliani, Governor George Pataki, and others to offer condolences to the individuals and families as they walked out of the building and boarded the chartered buses. I was touched by the breadth of human compassion, the significance of small expressions, thank you's, and the resiliency of humans in the midst of a tragedy. Many individuals, including Mayor Guliani and several priests, specifically sought me to thank me for participating and the remarks I made. I was, frankly, very surprised with this warm reception which I had not expected. (I wasn't sure what to expect.) During my remarks I had commented that we would be joining and offering prayers for the victims of the air tragedy.

The next day, on Monday, July the 22nd, I received a call from Rev. Stewart informing me that she had scheduled me for a special service being arranged for the 53 TWA members who died in the crash. This service was conducted on the evening of July 23rd, and over 500 employees and staff of TWA attended this service. Mr. J. Erickson, Chief Executive Officer of TWA, along with other religious leaders - bishops, rabbis, chaplains, etc. - were very thankful for our participation. Several employees of TWA, after the services, commented on the very special and good feelings they developed for Muslims after extensive travels in Muslim countries.

On Friday, July 25, 1996, I shared this experience with Muslims during the *Khutba*. Mr. D. McCue, editor of the local *Westbury Times*, reported on this as a lead story of the August 1st issue of the *Westbury Times* titled: "Westbury Mosque Holds TWA Memorial. Prayers for the Victims of Air Tragedy/Media Coverage Receives Scrutiny." Over 1,000 congregants attended. At the conclusion I asked for Allah's help for all who had been touched by the plane crash.

From this experience I have realized that there is a ground swell of good will amongst non-Muslims for Muslims. We, as a community, are not connected with the key individuals, organizers, or institutions. It was only at the initiative of Br. Hooper of CAIR that we were able to participate in this important event on Long Island. In retrospect, it is obvious that if the JFK Chaplains' Office had known about a Muslim organization or individual, we would have been a part of the process from the beginning. The irony is that a major Islamic center has been in operation for years and is less than five minutes from JFK.

We need to increase our efforts in reaching out to non-Muslims in educational, and public and private institutions; greater the linkages, better will be the interaction amongst the groups. We need to change from a spectator mode to a participant mode. Opportunities are there; are we willing to make the sacrifices?

Amongst the many positive spin-offs from this interaction was the contact we developed with the chaplains at JFK Airport, who have invited us to work with them in developing an organized Muslim presence at JFK - Insha Allah.

The lessons learned from this tragedy were of immense benefit when the next tragedy occurred in 1999. Before we recapitulate the Muslims' response to EgyptAir Flight 990 crash on October 21, 1999, we reproduce the news report summarizing the ICLI involvement in the TWA crash and the note of appreciation from the CEO, Mr. Jeffrey H. Erickson, of TWA.

The Westbury Times

Westbury Mosque Holds TWA Memorial Prayers for the Victims of Air Tragedy/Media Coverage Receives Scrutiny
By Daniel J. McCue

Nearly 1,000 worshippers convened at the Islamic Center of Long Island Friday afternoon for a memorial service in honor of the 230 victims of the crash of TWA Flight 800 off East Moriches, Long Island.

Since the fiery crash, which occurred shortly after 8:30 p.m. on July 16, religious leaders from the Islamic Center have participated in the two principal interfaith services, held both on the East End of the Island and at the Ramada Inn at Kennedy Airport.

In addition, doctors who are members at the center, most if not all affiliated with the Islamic Medical Association, have offered their aid and assistance to the recovery effort still under way out at sea, and to the families and friends of the victims.

But amidst the heartfelt prayers and recitations from the Holy Koran, the condolences offered to victims' families, and thanks offered to the emergency personnel who responded to the scene, was a palpable sense of anxiety and déjà vu.

For the American Muslim community, mysterious tragedies such as the one that occurred over the Atlantic two weeks ago serve to point up the lingering suspicion with which they are viewed in this country.

"We still don't know what happened to TWA Flight 800,"Dr. Faroque Khan told the assembled worshipers on Friday, only hours after the initial examination of the recovered flight data recorders proved inconclusive on the cause of the crash.

"If it was an accident, some kind of mechanical malfunction, then God willing, we must seek to find ways to prevent that kind of accident from occurring again. "If it was sabotage, then let us make clear that whoever did it had nothing to do with religion," Dr. Khan continued. "Taking innocent lives has nothing to do with faith."

For several years now, members of the Islamic Center have been attempting to improve the way followers of the Muslim faith are portrayed in the media. They have been particularly stung by how practitioners of terrorism in the Middle East and elsewhere have routinely been described as "Muslim" or "Islamic" terrorists.

Following the Oklahoma City bombing a year and a half ago, several newspapers and television and radio stations reported that the suspects were "Middle Eastern-looking men, and for a time, a man of Middle Eastern background was held in New York.

Though a young American, Timothy McVey, and two co-conspirators were eventually apprehended and are about to be tried for the crime, many Muslims felt unfairly singled out by the press.

Locally, the Islamic Center even received threatening phone calls after the Oklahoma explosion, and somebody attempted to shatter the Mosque's windows with a pellet gun.

According to Ghazi Y. Khankan, Interfaith Director for the Islamic Center of Long Island, similar Muslim-bashing began almost immediately after the Paris-bound TWA flight ended in a fire ball.

Among those he criticizes for their coverage are "The New York Times", "The New York Post," and several local television stations.

"First there was the plane crash, and then, even before any evidence was recovered, almost immediately there was talk of Pan Am Flight 103, the World Trade Center, and the attack on the military housing project in Saudi Arabia," Mr. Khankan said.

"It was as if people like the Times' A.M. Rosenthal, who wrote of the disaster in his "On My Mind" column of July 23, were deliberately trying to achieve some linkage between incidents. Such groundless speculation is extremely harmful to the bonds of relationship and trust that must exist between people in a society."

Mr. Khankan also had harsh words for many of those the media has relied on as "security experts" in their coverage of the crash.

"Following the plane crash, President Clinton came out and said, "We simply don't know what caused this tragedy," and he cautioned people about jumping to any conclusions.

"Unfortunately, his principled stand is not being mirrored by some members of the media and by some of these so-called "security experts," who are offering unsubstantiated claims of responsibility, unsourced com-

mentary, and raw speculation hinting at links between the tragedy and Arabs and Muslims.

Outside the main room of the Mosque, in the vestibule where worshippers remove their shoes, was a long table upon which had been left copies of a letter being sent to "The New York Times" and other media outlets. They essentially amplified the view of Mr. Khankan and other area Muslims. Pens were left nearby for worshippers who wished to add their signatures to the protest.

At the conclusion of his remarks at the service, Dr. Khan asked for God's help for all who have been touched by the plane crash and offered his fellow Muslims a bit of advice.

"Give us the wisdom..." he said, "to continue the real Jihad...the pursuit of self-improvement."

Excerpt of Note of Appreciation
From TWA CEO, Mr. Jeffrey H. Erickson
November 21, 1996
Dear Dr. Khan,
On behalf of the family of TWA employees, thank you for generously sharing your ecclesiastical gifts during the memorial service on July 21, Your generous spiritual leadership enabled people of all faiths to enjoy a measure of comfort during a time of great sorrow. It is with profound gratitude that I thank you for offering your expert guidance so grieving families, friends and TWA employees could begin to heal and cope with a tragedy beyond understanding. Thank you for keeping us in your prayers.

Sincerely,

Jeffrey H. Erickson

EgyptAir Flight 990 - October 31, 1999

This time the Muslim community at ICLI was better prepared, resulting from the experience gained from the TWA crash of 1996, and the fact that the majority of the passengers on this EgyptAir flight were Muslims, including five individuals whose families attended ICLI.

The morning of Sunday, October 31st, when the flight was reported missing, several members of the ICLI governing body – Board and Executive Committee – visited the Elzanaty and Abelmoneim families.

After the reports of the crash were confirmed, several members of ICLI went to JFK Airport to make themselves available to the families of the passengers, to the administrations of NYC and JFK Airport, and to the media to give them information and background regarding the Muslim practice of dealing with death. This presence was widely reported and appreciated by the media.

Excerpt from CNN.COM
Families of Flight 990 Passengers Flying From New York to Egypt October 31, 1999
Counselors, Muslim clerics helping families

Two Muslim religious leaders arrived Saturday at the Ramada Inn at John F. Kennedy International Airport in New York to console relatives of passengers who may have perished aboard the plane.

Ghazi Khankan, Imam of the Islamic Center of Long Island in Westbury, New York, told CNN that the parents of one of his center's members were on board the EgyptAir flight. Khankan said the parents lived in Egypt and were returning home after a visit to their son on Long Island.

As Khankan went into the Ramada to console grieving family members, he explained how people in the Muslim faith try to accept the death of loved ones.

"Death to us is a natural way, part of life," he said. "We are educated to feel patience and we are ordered to be patient under these circumstances. The moment we are born, God knows when we will die."

A Muslim cleric, from the Islamic Cultural Center in Manhattan, and grief counselors were also at the airport to comfort families.

This presence of Muslims at JFK, right from the beginning of this tragedy, was a big improvement over the tentative, hesitant response to the TWA Flight 800 crash in 1996. ICLI also arranged for special services on the evening of Sunday, October 31, 1999. These services received extensive coverage on local television, with all channels carrying excerpts of the services and interviews with the family members. This coverage also continued on national radio – NPR, and wire services reproduced segments of the coverage in local newspapers across the country. By being engaged and prepared, ICLI was able to fill a big void and provide the proper Muslim perspective to this human tragedy. I recall on Monday,

November 1st, I was engaged in continuous, nonstop interviews with the press, TV, and radio for several hours. These reporters had "camped out"at ICLI. On Tuesday, November 2, 1999, Newsday's lead story, with pictures of the passengers from Long Island, dealt with this crash and the role played by ICLI. Questions kept coming up - What about burial services? How do Muslims deal with natural disasters? Was this an accident or sabotage? To put a closure to these inquiries, ICLI management decided to have special services titled Remembering The Passengers of EgyptAir Flight 990 on Sunday, November 6, 1999, Rajab 27, 1420. These services included readings from the Quran, followed by some comments by the family members. As spokesperson of ICLI, I made the following remarks. This was followed by supplications, and the family members of the passengers met with friends, media personnel, and sympathizers – Muslim and non-Muslims, and all were appreciative of the opportunity provided by ICLI.

REMEMBERING THE PASSENGERS
OF EGYPTAIR FLIGHT 990

ISLAMIC CENTER OF LONG ISLAND
Saturday, November 6, 1999
Rajab 27, 1420

FAROQUE A. KHAN
Spokesperson, Islamic Center of Long Island

A week ago, last Saturday, 217 individuals boarded EgyptAir Flight 990 - 32 from Los Angeles, the rest at JFK. The plane was delayed and left from JFK after midnight. Shortly afterwards, contact was lost and the plane and passengers/crew apparently crashed into the Atlantic Ocean in the early morning hours of Sunday, October 31, 1999. All aboard are presumed dead.

Inna lillahi wa Inna ilayhi Rajiuun.
To Allah (God) we belong and to Him is our return.

Who was on the plane?
Gulad Mohd 12, Waller Said 19, Samah 15, Ahmed Aboshamah 13 - four exchange students returning home after two weeks of schooling and socializing as guests of families in Baltimore, MD.

One can only imagine the grief of the parents and siblings of these four promising youngsters.

Several tourists, travelers who liked to explore the world - from many parts of the USA.

Thirty-two high-ranking Egyptian military officers were returning after a period of observation and study in the USA. Breadwinners leave behind grieving families, children, spouses.

Newlyweds Richard Brokaw 76 and Virginia Chaplin 72.

Dr. Adel Elkosy, and his wife Wafaa, Chief of Radiology, VA Hospital, Chillicothe, Ohio. His 11 Christian staff remembered him fondly, used to celebrate holidays together, was so appreciative of the USA rights and freedom that he and his wife completed absentee ballots before leaving for the two-month journey last Friday. Before leaving, Dr. Elkousy embraced his apprehensive employees. His Administrative Assistant was crying and he reassured her with the words: "I am going home."

Inna lillahi wa Inna ilayhi Rajiuun.
To Allah we belong and to Him is our return.

Closer to home, on board flight 900 were:
Hisham, Tarek, Manah and Moha Elzanaty's parents
- Abdou and Fawqia, married 47 years
Dr. Talaat Abelmoneim's parents
- Abdel-Rahman and Alia

79

Wadida Farid's brother
- Captain Ahmed El Habashy, 57, who was a regular visitor to New York. He leaves behind three children.

Sharon and Bob Fitzpatrick from Long Island who enjoyed teaching and traveling.

On Flight 990 we had a cross-section of society - students, tourists, government officials, visitors returning back to Egypt, crew members, men and women, Muslims and non-Muslims, young and old - all called back by the Creator in a sudden quick way.

We, as humans, struggle and try to understand and cope and ask "Why?" These incidents put one's faith to an ultimate test. We take solace in the fact that we have no control over this. Our life here on earth is probation. We are tested by many things - calamities and some by good things. If we pass our probation with success, we are assured *Allah's* mercy in the Hereafter.

Some question about the Hereafter. We, as humans, need to recognize the limitations of our knowledge. For example, if four hundred years back someone from Long Island went to the beach and looked at the Atlantic Ocean, he or she would have no idea that an entire civilization lived across the other side of the ocean in Europe/Asia. Now we have no difficulties with understanding and accepting this because we have seen ourselves. Others have described it to us. Muslims believe in the Hereafter. Why? Because the *Quran* says so.

As Muslims we believe in the word of *Allah*, transmitted to Prophet Mohd and recorded in the *Quran*, and accept the guidelines and the facts regarding the *Dunya* (Here) and the *Akhira* (Hereafter).

We, at this time, pray for the families and relatives of the deceased. May *Allah* give them patience and strength to bear their loss.

We pray for the individuals who are trying to recover the remains of the departed and find the cause of the crash.

We pray for the departed passengers and crew.

I conclude with a quotation from the *Quran* and *Bible*.

> *Quran: Sura 4 V 78:*
> *Wherever ye are,*
> *Death will find you out,*
> *Even if ye are in towers*
> *Built up strong and high!*

> *Bible: John 3:8*
> *Jesus reminds Nicodemus*
> *The wind bloweth where it healeth,*
> *and those hearest the sound thereof,*
> *but can not tell whence it cometh and*
> *whither it goeth.*

How do Muslims view death?

Like Jews and Christians, Muslims believe that the present life is only a trial preparation for the next realm of existence. Basic articles of faith include: the Day of Judgement, resurrection, Heaven and Hell. When a Muslim dies, he or she is washed, usually by a family member, wrapped in a clean white cloth, and buried with a simple prayer preferably the same day. Muslims consider this one of the final services they can do for their relatives, and an opportunity to remember their own brief existence here on earth. The Prophet (SAW) taught that three things can continue to help a person even after death; charity which he/she had given, knowledge which he/she had imparted, and prayers on their behalf by a righteous child.

Lessons Learned From TWA Flight 800 and EgyptAir Flight 990 Tragedies

1. There is a groundswell and untapped good will for Muslims amongst non-Muslims in North America.

2. The vast majority of non-Muslims in North America have very little information regarding Islam and Muslims. A simple fact like Muslims' belief and reverence for ALL prophets from Adam to Mohammed - peace and blessings of Allah be upon all of them - is news for a large majority of non-Muslims.

3. The Muslim community, by and large, is disconnected from major news and opinion-molding institutions in the USA.

4. Once a structure for disseminating accurate information is developed - as was done at ICLI, the news media is willing and forthcoming to get the news regarding Muslims, about Muslims, from Muslims.

5. There is a great and urgent need for the Muslim community, in particular institutions, cultural centers, masajids, and Islamic centers to develop local, regional and, eventually, national networks.

Chapter 9

WOMEN IN THE MOSQUE:
"Why do Muslims treat women so poorly?"

In any discussion between Muslims and non-Muslims, this question is very likely to come up. To understand and address this very contemporary question, one must know the four distinct phases of the growth of Islam.

First is the seventh-century Arab society in which the religion of Islam was established. The second phase is that of the early centuries of Islam, beginning with the advent of the holy book, the *Quran*, and the teachings of the Prophet Muhammad (PBUH). These were the basis for the Islamic religious, social and political movements as it fanned out in all directions from its Arab homeland.

The third phase is the period of great decline (1250-1900). It is in this long period, following the political and physical disasters accompanying those tribal movements of fierce nomads from the East, that the picture of woman's role in Islamic society began to deteriorate.

The fourth and final period is the contemporary period of resurgence from the late nineteenth century to the present day. This was partly due to influence from Europe and America coinciding with an awakening within the Muslim world. Well-known writer and activist, Jamal al Din al Afghani, his student Muhammad Abdul, and others like Qasim Amin, included reforms in the treatment of women in their movements.

Some Basic Guidelines From The *Quran* And *Hadith* Regarding The Role Of Women In Islam:

- More than 1400 years ago Islam eliminated the chattel status of women, prohibited the pre-Islamic practice of female infanticide and gave women full control over their earnings and wealth.
- Other rights granted to women by Islam include the right of inheritance, the right to initiate divorce and the right to own a business. The Prophet Muhammad's wife Khadijah was a prosperous businesswoman. She initiated the marriage proposal.

82

- The first martyr in Islam was a woman, as was the first person to accept the Prophet's message from God.
- According to the *Quran*, Islam's revealed text: "The believers, men and women, are protectors, one of another..." (*Quran* 9:71)
- The Prophet Muhammad, himself, said: "Whoever has a daughter and does not bury her alive (the pre-Islamic practice forbidden by Islam), does not insult her, and does not favor his son over her, God will enter him into Paradise."

A few illustrative examples:

<u>Ayesha Siddiqa</u> - Leader and Teacher

Ayesha, wife of Prophet Muhammad (PBUH), was a teacher for both men and women. Her students taught others how to govern, how to organize Muslim communities, how to arrange Muslim family and social life. At time of crisis, she took command of the Islamic army, leading it in the field of battle. In peacetime she was a treasured resource for all regarding the teachings of Islam and the traditions of the Prophet Muhammad (PBUH).

<u>Asma bint Abu Bakr</u>

Asma is famous for the role she played at the time of Hijrah when Prophet Muhammad and his close companion Abu Bakr escaped from Mecca to Medina. They did not have anything to tie up the food required for the arduous journey in the desert. Asma tore up her waistband into two pieces. One she kept to tie her dress, and with the other she tied up the food required for the journey. Asma, for this innovation, used to be referred to as *zat-in-nitaqqain* (she of the two waistbands).

There are many incidents and stories related to the role women played during the early history of Islam in all aspects of life. Women participated in war. During the battle of Marj as Safar when Muslims were fighting the Romans, Umm Hakeem was involved in close combat and is reported to have killed seven Roman soldiers. Women were engaged in public policy and debate. There is a famous story about a woman who held a heated argument with the caliph Umar over the reduction and limitation of dowries. After she rose in the mosque and presented her views, the caliph bowed to the lady in admiration and declared his acceptance of the validity of her case.

The *Quran's* insistence on equality for the sexes and emphasis on education brought many benefits. Women became poets, writers, and leaders in diverse fields. Sukayanah (d 735 AC), daughter of Husayn ibn Ali, was a leader in fashion, beauty and literature. Rabiah al Adawiyyah was one of the most famous Sufi poets. These women of early Islam were not veiled. Islam taught them propriety, but they were never told to live lives of segregation and isolation. From the following passage, it's clear that the Quran imposes on both men and women the same sense of modesty.

> *Quran: 24:30-31*
> *Say to the believing men that they should lower their gaze and guard their modesty; that will make for greater purity for them: And Allah is well acquainted with all that they do.*
>
> *And say to the believing women that they should lower their gaze and guard their modesty; that they should not display their beauty and ornaments except what (must ordinarily) appear thereof: that they should draw their veils over their bosoms and not display their beauty except to their husbands, their fathers, their husbands' fathers, their sons, their husbands' sons, their brothers' or their brothers' sons.*
>
> *Or their sisters' sons, or their women, or the slaves whom their right hands possess, or male servants free of physical needs, or small children who have no sense of the shame of sex; and that they should not strike their feet in order to draw attention to their hidden ornaments. And O ye Believers! Turn ye all together towards Allah, that ye may attain Bliss.*

The reader quite correctly is wondering if the above was the state of affairs regarding the women in early Islam, then what happened? Why is it that most Muslim women in the world are uneducated, segregated, isolated, and generally not engaged in the affairs of the community. To understand this state of affairs, many explanations are possible. Most scholars feel the decline started with the Mongol invasion in 1250, and the long period following the political and physical disasters accompanying those tribal movements of fierce nomads from the East that the picture of woman's role in Islam society began to deteriorate. Lamya al Faruqi, in her book *Women, Muslim Society and Islam*, Trust publication 1988, offers the following explanation:

> ***Social Affairs:*** *It is in her social role that the degradation of many Muslim women of this period has been most notorious. Everyone has read of the profligate concubinage and polygamy, as well as the veiled prisoners of the harem. Despite the fact that concubinage had been forbidden, that polygamy had been regulated and discouraged, and that the early Muslims had not condoned such customs as the harem, purdah, and the veil, these practices which revealed woman's subordinate role in life have been associated with Islam and Islamic culture by many Muslims as well as non-Muslims who did not bother to know the facts about the religion, who were given misleading information, or who knew only this one period of Islam's history. Though the society did not revert to the horrible pre-Islamic practice of female infanticide, the birth of a girl to any family was considered a misfortune to be mourned, the birth of a boy a blessing to be celebrated. And no wonder! For the lot of the girl was in most cases that of a second class citizen who did not receive an adequate education to prepare her for anything but the role of household servant. Her role as wife and mother was only inadequately filled, for she was not educated sufficiently to care for more than the barest physical needs of her children and husband. It gradually became the rule that women had no function in life beyond the immediate family circle inside the home. Though Islam, realizing the human need for a mother's care, had given women stronger custody rights over children than their fathers, these rights were gradually left unclaimed; and custody, except in unusual cases where the religious courts stepped in to reverse the practice, was automatically given to the male side of the family.*

What went wrong? What happened that made woman

become ashamed of her sex, that made her retire to a position of weakness and subservience to the male in these later centuries of Islam?

Many explanations are possible. Perhaps no one of them is exclusively responsible. Political upheavals as devastating as the Turkish and Mongol invasions were, are bound to produce a shock of widespread effect in the culture. And it was in fact this shock that forced the culture into a period of conservatism which grew steadily stronger as that culture sought to maintain its equilibrium under the impact of the new influences from outside. Feudalism may have been a second cause for the deterioration of women's rights. As the problems of security increased, as the original unity of the Islamic ummah or community splintered, as wealth was gradually concentrated in the hands of fewer and fewer people, the Islamic society sank into a feudalistic period from which, in some lands, it did not completely escape up to the present day.

A third explanation of the reversal of the rights Islam had won for women is that they were the result of the change which occurs when a tribal society moves to a foreign or urban environment. While a tribal people lives its life among known relatives or friends, there were few dangers to the preservation of the tribe's exclusiveness, its normal kinship patterns, and the control of its members. But as these tribal and country people moved to new lands and to urban areas, this control was endangered and the society instinctively began protecting its women with great care. It was then that the Muslims took on the Persian and Byzantine customs of the face veil and the harem. Women were gradually forced into a more and more secluded and oppressed life.

A fourth explanation is that after the weakening of the initial strength of the Islamic movement the basic customs and practices of the areas where Islam had brought its message began to reassert themselves in opposition to the beliefs and principles of the Quranic teaching. Whichever of these causes is responsible or whatever other causes combined to produce an unfavorable reversal of the Islamic advance in regard to the status of women, we know that by the late nineteenth century her situation was in crying need of reform.

Reform Period (1900-Present)
Then in the late nineteenth century a period of reform began. This was partly due to influences from Europe and America, where the liberalizing influences of the Enlightenment period, as well as the Industrial Revolution with its need for women to be included in the work force, had brought about revolutionary changes in the thinking about women's status, if not always concrete results. It was also due to an awakening from within the Muslim world. Reformers in various countries began advocating a new look at women's rights. The well-known writer and activist Jamal al Din al Afghani and his student Muhammad Abdul included reforms in the treatment of women in their movements. Qasim Amin was another active leader in the movement for emancipation of women as viewed from within the Islamic context.

The following example from the four generations of the author's family will highlight the status and the evolving role of Muslim women during the past century.

Khurshaappa:
Author's grandmother, born in 1879 in Kashmir, died 1962, did not receive any formal education.

Sara:
Author's mother, born in 1905 in Kashmir, died 1980, received formal education until fifth grade.

Misra Maryam Rayhana:
Author's sister, born in 1925 in Kashmir, received formal education until tenth grade.

Mumtaz Anwar:
Author's sister, born in 1940 in Kashmir, graduated from medical school, practicing physician.

Shireen Khan:
Author's daughter, born in 1973 in New York, completing Masters in Child Psychology.

The formal limited education of the author's grandmother, mother and older sister was a result of the environment in which they lived. Their desire for education was as strong as that of the women born after 1940 when schooling became available in safe neighborhoods and transportation modalities improved. The message is very obvious - environment determines the degree of education Muslim women receive. The experience in the author's family is being repeated all over the world.

Women at Islamic Center of Long Island:

During the development of ICLI's bylaws, it was stipulated that both women and men will serve on the governing body. Since 1984, every two years, women and men contest in the elections for the various positions on the Executive Committee. In addition, a number of important committees are chaired and staffed by women. Although this is now a well-established practice at ICLI, the practice is not uniformly followed in other centers. The following article from *Newsday* summarizes the role women play in managing the activities at ICLI.

Woman Perseveres To Serve Mosque
***Newsday*, August 1, 1993**

As the recently elected vice president of the Islamic Center of Long Island in Westbury, Dr. Arfa Khan is the highest ranking woman official in Nassau County mosques.

Neither the Ta Ha Mosque in Roosevelt, nor the Islamic Center of the South Shore in Valley Stream, has any women in executive positions.

Khan said that some members of the Muslim community objected to having a woman in office, and even challenged as "un-Islamic" the by-laws of the Westbury mosque that mandate that at least one woman be on the five-member executive committee. Once the board of trustees, which includes two women, met with the protesters, however, the objections stopped.

"Women have a very high place in the Koran (the Muslim holy book). Spiritually and morally, women are equal to men. No one's superior or inferior," Khan said. She added, "I have worked with men since the inception of the mosque. There is no way that women can be excluded. We built the mosque together."

Leading the fund-raising effort, Khan, 49, was instrumental in the construction of an entirely new mosque, complete with a high dome and marble floors. The Westbury mosque is the first such building to be erected on Long Island. Before, the center operated out of a house, which is now behind the new building.

Despite her multiple demanding duties as chief of thoracic radiology and director of body CAT scan at Long Island Jewish Medical Center in New Hyde Park, and Professor of Radiology at Albert Einstein College of Medicine in the Bronx, Khan made time to be an active member of the Westbury mosque since its founding in 1984.

She was one of the mosque's first treasurers, and was chairwoman of the fund-raising committee for many years. She took office as vice president July 1. Her term, which is unpaid, runs two years.

Being in a position to do so, Khan said she especially wants "to educate Americans about Islam." As an advocate of interfaith dialoguing, she said, "I want (the mosque) to be a center for everyone, Muslims and non-Muslims, to learn about the religion."

In light of recent ties of a group of Muslims to the World Trade Center bombing and the alleged plot to bomb other locales in New York City, Khan said, "Muslims are always associated with violence, with terrorism. When you have one billion Muslims in the world, sure, some of them are bad guys, but not all of them." "It is important to hear different perspectives," she continued. "As vice president, I hope I can help change the distorted perception of Muslims."

Khan and her husband, Faroque, the chief of medicine at Nassau County Medical Center, moved from Kashmir to the United States 23 years ago. They were classmates in medical school in Kashmir and decided to marry in their third year. Their "love marriage" created a stir on a campus where couples were usually the consequence of parental arrangements, Khan said.

The two now live in Muttontown and have two children. Their son, Arif, is 26 and graduated from Yale Medical School. Their daughter, Shireen, is 20 and plans to pursue a career in child psychology.

A U.S. citizen since 1975, Khan said she encourages Muslims, especially women, to "get involved and take advantage of all the opportunities in this country." She added, "Staying at home is boring."

To answer the frequently asked question regarding the role of women in Islam, Dr. Lamya al Faruqi succinctly responds to this question as follows:

Islam brought women from the position of chattel in marriage to that of equal partners. In the matter of divorce, she changed from a completely impotent bystander, to one who could initiate divorce proceedings and claim her rights of dowry and inheritance. From a position of legal nonentity, she became a legal personality in the full sense of the term, able to hold property, entitled to a just share of her husband's and family's inheritance property. Socially, with education equally required of her as well as of every man in Islam, she rose to a position of social and cultural influence and service. Even in religio-cultic practices and duties, woman was asked and expected to play a role equal to that of man, insofar as her special physical characteristics and maternal duties allowed. Her position in early Islam was really an exemplary one, one that should be studied and known by every woman as well as every liberationist in the twentieth century - in America as well as in the Muslim world. The Muslim woman, if she is true to the principles of her religion, has lessons in equality to teach the Westerner, and her descendants in the East have to learn anew the role demanded of them by their religion. Orientalists and Orientals zealous for modernization should cease to put the blame on Islam, a blame which instead deserves to fall on their own ignorance of the faith and on the political and social decline which their nations suffered in the past.

At ICLI our goal is to have women and men live and practice up to their full potential.

Chapter 10

ROLE OF MASJID, FRIDAY PRAYERS, ETIQUETTE AND CONTENT OF *KHUTBAHS*

ROLE OF MASJID

The word *masjid* is derived from the root *Sajdah*, which translates into adoration, prostration; hence, *masjid* is used for the place of performing *Sajdah* - an act of utmost humility and adulation in the presence of the supreme source.

On the basis of the Quranic logic, as a rule, all living beings bow as an act of submission and prostrate before the Almighty:

> *Have they not regarded all things that God has created casting their shadows to the right and to the left, prostrating themselves before God in all lowliness? Before God prostrate everything in the heavens, and every creature crawling on the earth, and the angels. They do now wax proud. (16:48-49) An-Nahl*

Historically, two important mosques served as the starting point and the end or the destination of the intellectual and spiritual voyage of the Prophet Muhammed (PBUH). The words "voyage" and "movement" occurring in the Quranic verses convey a vast range of meaning:

> *Glory to (Allah) Who did take His servant for a journey by night from the sacred mosque to the farthest mosque whose precincts We did bless - in order that We might show him some of Our signs: for He is the One Who heareth and seeth (all things). Sura 17 Verse 1*

On his way to *al Medinah*, while migrating from Mecca, as soon as the Prophet(s) reached a place known as *Quba*, he laid the foundation of a mosque there, known as *Masjid Quba*, which is now among the holy places of Muslims. This was the first step towards the formation of a small Muslim society. To briefly review the features of a mosque -

91

Salient Features

1. Sanctity as a mosque.
2. Pivot of cultural and spiritual movement.
3. Pivot for social movement.

Sanctity

A mosque is free of decorations. All such things which interferes with a man's/woman's communion with God in word, action, thought should be discarded before entering a mosque - and a state of perfect physical and spiritual purity maintained. Upkeep and maintenance of the mosque is incumbent upon Muslims. It is stated that the Prophet Mohd. (PBUH) said: *Whoever sweeps a mosque on Thursday night, cleaning it of (as little as) a speck of dust is forgiven.*

Cultural and Spiritual Movement

During the Prophet's time and afterwards, mosques fulfilled both function of purification of the soul and acquisition of knowledge.

Social Movement

A mosque is a place for performing all duties in the way of God. All social, cultural and political activities which are religiously oriented should be launched from the mosque.

During Prophet Mohd.'s (PBUH) stay in Medinah, the mosque served as a center of all cultural and political bustle. Besides worship and spiritual retirement, many social and political events were discussed and planned. This practice was continued during the time of the righteous caliphs.

Traditionally, the largest congregation of Muslims occurs for Friday congregational prayers, and it's useful to review the background of the development and the traditions followed in this congregational gathering.

ETIQUETTE OF FRIDAY PRAYERS

Sura Al-Jumua or the Assembly - Sura 62 Verse 9
O ye who believe! When the call is proclaimed to prayer
on Friday, hasten earnestly to the remembrance of Allah,
and leave off business.

Friday prayer was established by the Prophet (PBUH), himself, without any command for it from the *Quran*. This is further proof of the place of the *Sunnah* in Islam. It shows that whatever the Prophet (PBUH) orders or establishes is part of the religion, regardless of whether it is mentioned in the *Quran* or not.

Sura 62 Verse 11
But when they see some bargain or some pastime, they
disperse and leave thee standing and say, "That which
Allah has is better than pastime or bargain. And Allah is
best to provide."

In Maulana Maududis introduction and explanation of *Sura Al-Jumua* 62, he explains: The second section (vv 9-11) was sent down shortly after the emigration, for the Holy Prophet (upon whom be *Allah's* peace) who had established the Friday congregational Prayer on the fifth day after his arrival at Madinah. The incident that has been referred to in this verse must have occurred at a time when the people had not yet received full training in the etiquette of religious congregations.

This section was sent down on an occasion when a trade caravan arrived in Madinah right at the time of the Friday congregational service, and hearing its din and drum the audience, except for 12 men, left the Prophet's mosque and rushed out to the caravan, although the Holy Prophet (upon whom be *Allah's* peace) at that was delivering the sermon. Thereupon it was enjoined that after the call is sounded for the Friday Prayer all trade and business and other occupations become forbidden. The believers should then suspend every kind of transaction and hasten to the remembrance of *Allah*. However, when the Prayer is over, they have the right to disperse in the land to resume their normal occupations.

The Friday Prayer is a duty and <u>obligation</u> upon every Muslim in the community except: a slave, a woman, a child, a sick person, a traveler.

Umar Ibn al Khattab saw a man dressed for traveling and he heard him say, "If today were not Friday, I would have left." Umar responded, "Go, for Friday should not keep one from traveling."

GENERAL PRINCIPLES

Attire

Prophet disapproved of wearing silk for men, preferring using white color.

Principle

Any time a Muslim intends to attend a public gathering, he/she should do his/her best to cleanse themselves and make his/her presence presentable. Avoid using raw garlic or onions. This is out of respect for others.

Timing

Going early: By leaving early for Friday Prayers one gets the reward of waiting for the prayer, making *dhikr* (remembering *Allah*) and voluntary prayers during that time. Practice of Prophet was to perform prayer either before or after zenith of the sun - sometimes before *dhur* started, sometimes after *dhur* started. However, the prayer must be completed <u>before ASR.</u>

Ghusl (Bath) *Hadith* - Bukhari and Muslim

Ghusl for Friday Prayer is recommended *(Sunnah)*. Hazrat Aisha, wife of Prophet (PBUH) said, "People would come from their houses and outskirts of Madinah. They used to pass through dust and be drenched with sweat and covered with dust. Sweat used to pour from them. One of them came to the Prophet (PBUH) who said, "I wish you would clean yourself on this day of yours."

HOW TO GET TO THE MOSQUE
Walk to the Mosque

Hadith: "Whoever makes *ghusl* on Friday, goes early, walks to the mosque (does not ride - camels/cars) comes close to the Imam, listens and does not speak uselessly. Then for every step he/she takes, he/she will have the reward of a year's worth of fasting and praying. This very relevant advice from 1,400 years ago has a lot of relevance for Muslims in North America today.

Muslims need to establish homes near mosques. Thereby, they will strengthen the community, become more visible and active in community affairs, and have an impact on society-at-large. Those who drive to the mosque, preferably need to park in <u>designated</u> areas outside and inside the premises, and gain the extra rewards and benefits of walking to the mosque. This habit will also increase the acceptability of Muslims amongst their non-Muslim neighbors.

Inside Mosque

Hadith - Abu Dawud, etc.: Prophet (PBUH) saw a man stepping over people in the mosque while he was giving *Khutbah.* He said, "Sit down. You have harmed the people and come late."

Adhan (literal meaning of which is making known, notification, announcement): During the Prophet's (PBUH) time, only one *Adhan* was called when the Prophet (PBUH) sat on the minbar, the same tradition was followed during the time of Abu Bakr and Omar's time. During the third caliphate – Uthman's time, after the number of Muslims increased, second call was added in the marketplace and not inside the mosque.

Sunnah: Prayers:	<u>Before Friday:</u>	Free to pray whatever one wishes on a voluntary basis.
	<u>After Friday:</u>	May pray either two or four *rakats* based on Prophet (PBUH) actions or statements.

The goal of proper etiquette during Friday Prayers is to help all Muslims perform the very important Friday Prayer in the proper manner, in the manner most pleasing to *Allah.*

95

WHY IS FRIDAY PRESCRIBED FOR MUSLIMS?

Hadith - Bukhari and Muslims

The messenger of *Allah* (PBUH) said, "Whoever makes ablution and excels in performing it, then goes to the mosque and <u>listens</u> and <u>remains</u> quiet, then forgiven for him will be whatever he did (minor sins) from that Friday to the previous Friday plus three additional days.

Listening and remaining silent are expected.

In numerous *hadith* of the Prophet (PBUH), he made it abundantly clear that the members of the congregation must remain silent while the *Khateeb* is delivering the *Khutbah*.

The *Khateeb* is permitted to speak to members and for them to reply.

During the Prophet's (PBUH) *Khutbah*, man entered and sat down. The Prophet (PBUH) asked, "Did you pray two *rakats*?" Man said, "No." The Prophet (PBUH) told him, "Then stand and pray."

Khutbah

It is obligatory to listen to the *Khutbah* and those who intentionally miss it are sinners.

Basic *Pillars of Khutbah* include

1. Praising *Allah* at beginning.
2. Prayers upon the Prophet (PBUH).
3. Some admonition to *Taqwa*.
4. Verse from the *Quran* to be recited.
5. Some supplication or *dua*.

FINAL WORDS

The Friday Prayer is one of the most important acts of worship in Islam. Perhaps it would not be an exaggeration to say that the whole morning of Friday should be geared around preparing and going to the mosque for this special event that the Prophet (PBUH) has described as *Eid*.

However, the Prophet (PBUH) has also made it clear that not everyone who attends it receives the full benefits and blessings of this wonderful act. In one *Hadith*, the Prophet (PBUH) stated, "There are three types of people who attend the Friday Prayer. One is a man who is present but speaks [during the *Khutbah*] and that is his portion of the prayer. Second is a man who is present and makes supplications. In his case, *Allah* may give him what he asks, if He wishes, or He may not give him what he asks. Third is a person who is present and observes silence and does not step over the necks of the Muslims nor does he harm anyone. For him, there is expiation from that Friday until the previous Friday plus an additional three days."

In order to achieve full benefit of this wonderful Prayer, one should fulfill the following:

1. Make *ghusl*/bath.
2. Purifying and cleaning oneself.
3. Applying oil to one's hair - cleaning the hair and beard, making them presentable.
4. Use some perfume.
5. Upon going to the mosque, he/she must not separate two people who are sitting together. He/She also must not step over people to get to some place he/she wants to sit.
6. He/She prays as much as he/she wishes while waiting for the Imam to come.
7. He/She remains quiet while the Imam is delivering the *Khutbah*. This actually includes listening to the Imam and not playing with anything while the Imam is speaking. The goal is to put all his/her attention into what the Imam is saying.
8. Walking to the mosque is preferred over driving and parking appropriately is a MUST!
9. Not harming anyone while going to the mosque and while in the mosque. Indeed, it includes any kind of harmful act, even while one is on the way to the mosque.

10. While going to the mosque, he/she must be in a state of calmness and tranquility, not being hurried or rushed.
11. Sitting close to the Imam.
12. Avoiding the major sins during the remainder of the week.

TOPICS FOR THE FRIDAY *KHUTBAH*

At the Islamic Center of Long Island, under the overall supervision of Dr. Sultan Hameed, a format and structure for the Friday *Khutbahs* has evolved. The *Khateebs* represent various ethnic backgrounds, such as individuals from Arab, African, Asian, European background. This rotation schedule allows a presentation of diverse viewpoints and helps in making Muslims of all backgrounds and viewpoints welcome at ICLI.

I have been involved in the rotational schedule for the Friday *Khutbahs* since October 1995. In each of my presentations I have attempted to incorporate a current issue of concern to Muslims, and attempted to provide possible solutions based on my understanding of the *Al Quran* and the *Sunnah* of the Prophet (PBUH). Some of the topics I have covered in these presentations include:

- *Future of Muslims in North America*
- *Should Muslims Assimilate or Isolate From Mainstream Society?*
- *Challenges and Opportunities for Muslims in the USA*
- *Faith and Culture*
- *Addressing Most Commonly Asked Questions of Muslims by Non-Muslims:*
  a) Role of Prophets Such as Jesus Christ in Islam
  b) Role of Women in Islam
  c) Nation of Islam
  d) What Does Khilafah Mean?

98

During special months, such as *Ramadhan* and *Dhul Hijjah*, I reviewed the concept of fasting and the meaning of *Hajj*. There were occasions when the entire *Khutbah* had to be modified to address contemporary fast-moving news impacting Muslims. On July 26, 1996 my entire presentation focused on the crash of TWA Flight 800 and the way Muslims were affected and responding. This *Khutbah* was reported in the news media. On November 26, 1999, during the Thanksgiving holiday, my presentation addressed the topic *Concept of Thanksgiving in Islam*.

I reproduce portions of my *Khutbah* of December 31, 1999 in which I addressed the issues facing Muslims in America and provided some suggestions for possible solutions. This presentation was during the month of *Ramadhan*, and I attempted to incorporate the significance of *Ramadhan* with the importance of introspection and self-analysis.

STATE OF THE MUSLIM COMMUNITY IN THE USA

Friday, December 31, 1999 - Ramadhan 23rd 1420

Quran 2:183 - Baqarah
> *O ye who believe,*
> *Fasting is prescribed to you*
> *As it was prescribed to those before you*
> *That ye may (learn)*
> *Self restraint.*

A month of introspection, increased charity, enhanced family and community interaction, and enhanced spirituality - three things stand out during *Ramadhan*:

1. commemorate the beginning of Quranic revelation;
2. exercise in self-discipline, enhanced spirituality, and
3. feel hunger, thirst, and thereby gain a better appreciation of the needs of the poor and have-nots.

99

During the last 10 days, on an odd night we celebrate and commemorate *Al-Qadr*.

Sura 97 - Al-Qadr or The Night of Power.
1. *Lo! We revealed it on the Night of Power.*
2. *Ah, what will convey to thee what the Power is.*
3. *The Night of Power is better than a thousand months.*
4. *The angels and the Spirit descend therein, by the permission of their Lord, with all decrees.*
5. *(That night is) Peace until the rising of the dawn.*

This presentation, during this very special time of *Ramadhan*, is an introspection, analysis of the Muslim community here in Long Island/New York/the USA. What is our current status? What are the issues facing us? What do we need to do as a group to accomplish the goals within the guidelines set forth in *Al-Quran* and the *Sunnah of Prophet Mohammad* (PBUH)? What can each one of us do, as individuals, as families, and as a community?

Insha Allah, we are going to think, plan, and execute a plan together.

Some of you may wonder, "Why do all of this?" Doesn't *Allah* give and take as he pleases and chooses? In response, I would suggest that Muslims are encouraged to think, reflect, and plan; and after that's done, *Allah* will take care of the rest.

In *Al-Quran*, the word *Aqala* appears 50 times - it means "connect ideas together, reason, understand an intellectual argument." *Afala taqilun* appears 13 times - "Have ye then no sense?" People incapable of intellectual effort needed to cast off routine thinking are stigmatized as "a people of no intelligence."

Sura 3 Al-Imran - Verse 190.

> *Behold! In the creation of the heavens and the earth,*
> *And the alternation of Night and Day -*
> *There are indeed signs for men of understanding.*

It was reported by Abu Hurairah that Prophet Mohammad (PBUH) said, *Anyone who fasts in the month of Ramadhan with faith and engages in self evaluation will be forgiven his or her previous sins.*

Quran 25:44
Or thinkest thou that most of them listen or understand?
> *They are only like cattle; nay, they are worse astray in Path.*

Prophet's final sermon:

> *Reason well, therefore O people, and ponder my words which I now convey to you. I am leaving you with the Book of God and the Sunnah of His prophet. If you follow them, you will never go astray.*

So our exercise of critical self analysis at this Friday's *Khutbah* is something which our faith encourages us to do.

Prophet Mohammad (PBUH), during *Ramadhan*, used to perform *Atiqaf*, which is really a time of self analysis away from the hustle and bustle of daily life.

CRITICAL MASS

A few years back I asked Dr. Hassan Hathout about his impressions regarding the status of the Muslim community. His response was that after we reach a "critical mass" things will start happening. I don't think Dr. Hathout was referring to the numerical numbers. He was probably alluding to the involvement of Muslims in various phases and aspects of life in the USA. I believe we have reached that critical mass, and here are my reasons for stating this:

1. Numerical Count - Experience at ICLI and other communities all over the USA reflects this. We are being noticed.

2. Media Attention - During this month we have been the subject of several news and TV stories. December 5, 1999: Bob Keeler gave his impressions about issues which are testing and challenging the four influential faith groups Catholics/Jews/Protestants/Muslims. December 9, 1999: Month of *Ramadhan*. *Muslims Fast Feed Soul* - positive headline, picture of Dr. Rizvon at work showing faith in action. December 19, 1999: I gave a brief expose on *Ramadhan* on NBC. December 12, 1999: *Newsday* highlighted portraits of a century. A picture of ICLI was shown, along with first synagogue, AME Church, etc., showing that we have come a long, long way.

NATIONAL LEVEL

William J. Clinton

> *We look forward to the day when people of all faiths can freely express their beliefs without fear of persecution or discrimination. Each year, Ramadhan brings a promise of renewal and hope for the world. I pray that, as the new moon rises, we will witness the beginning of a new era of*

tolerance around the globe. As the followers of Islam celebrate the revelation of God's word to Muhammad, we join you in honoring his call for harmony and peace.

Secretary of State Madeline Albright hosted an *Iftar* party at the State Department. Next year the State Department plans to have an exhibit at the ISNA convention. They are looking for individuals who can give an Islamic perspective in the State Department.

We have noticed the presidential candidates mentioning mosques and Muslims and Islam when they talk about Abrahamic faiths.

On November 4, 1999 Congressman T. Davis (R-VA 11th) introduced a congressional resolution expressing *Sense of Congress*, that a postage stamp be issued recognizing *Ramadhan*.

Last, but not least, the traffic light outside ICLI, and an invitation to the inauguration of the new legislatures on Monday, January 3, 2000.

The community is evolving and maturing, and our experience in handling catastrophes such as the recent EgyptAir crash verifies this. December 30, 1999: *Newsday's* cover sheet had a selection of stories which had a major impact. EgyptAir is one of them, with Br. Hisham Elzanaty's quotation regarding his deceased parents.

PROBLEMS AND CHALLENGES

In my previous *Khutbahs* I have shared with you my impressions regarding issues facing the community. I will highlight a few of them today.

Our problem is not of numbers, but understanding. We need to make a leap from the mentality of the victim/persecuted to one of actively engaged citizens who are willing to work towards participation and empowerment, and not harp on exclusion and discrimination. If I were to pose a simple question of "Where is your home?" many would take a long time to reflect and then respond – the immigrant's ambivalence. As to my own response, I would agree with Dr. Hathout's definition. Home is NOT where our ancestors are buried, but where our grandchildren will be buried.

IMAGE AND STEREOTYPING

We are making progress, but there is still a lot of work to do. What will be the identity of Muslims in America? In Europe, they are treated as second-class: United Kingdom – Indians/Pakistanis, France – Algerians, Germany – Turks.

Here in the USA we have the freedom and opportunity to read, think critically, and hence make major contributions to *Ummah* from here. We can become the ambassadors to the Muslim world and be mobilized for grassroots diplomacy.

CIVIL RIGHTS: Citizenship, Equal Opportunity, and Equality Before the Law
Groups that have achieved civil rights here have made a major impact. We have a way to go in this - secret evidence, passenger profiling are examples where Muslims, specifically, are being targeted.

NOT A PART OF JUDEO-CHRISTIAN FRAMEWORK
Them Vs Us. In reality, Islam is closer to Judaism and Christianity than they are to one another. It's our job to educate the Jews and Christians about this.

WOMEN'S STATUS
There is mass confusion regarding this issue. It's our job to rectify this. Priorities are misplaced. For example, 30,000 women in Turkey are refused public education because of their choice to wear a headscarf – an example of secular tyranny.

More women take positions in the Iranian parliament than in the US Senate. Women hold positions of VP in the Iranian government. Women have been in leadership positions in Pakistan, Indonesia, Turkey, Bangladesh, etc. This fact and reality is ignored by the media.

VIOLENT RELIGION
Islam is often associated with terrorism. However, Islam has no room for terrorism. Those who blow up buildings and embassies, and hijack planes are not even human, and we condemn such actions as we condemn state terrorism - be it in Chechnya, Afghanistan, Iraq, Kashmir, or Kosova. The meaning and significance of *Jehad* has been misrepresented and fixed in the minds of non-Muslims. We need to correct this. However, we, I believe, have the means and knowledge to address them. In fact, the actions we take here at ICLI have an impact not only here, but literally around the world. I was browsing ICLI's Web page recently and share with you a few messages to amplify on my comment regarding ICLI's global impact.

One message, Can't believe there is such a mosque in New York.

HOW DO WE ADDRESS THESE ISSUES?

Reviewing historical examples might give us, and other Muslims, some guidance as to how Prophet Mohammad (PBUH) handled difficult situations and challenges.

BATTLE OF THE TRENCH

When Muslims were surrounded by a numerically much-larger force, the Prophet (PBUH) consulted with his companions. Salman, the Persian, suggested a new method of defense – they dug a trench around Medinah. Prophet accepted this. He was personally involved. There was a long siege; and after a very difficult period, the Muslims were eventually successful.

MESSAGE

Prophet adopted a strategy which was totally new for Arabs at that time. We need to keep our minds open to new techniques and methodology.

BATTLE OF BADR

Prophet (PBUH) was corrected by companions regarding war strategy. Message: Consult, seek advice. No on, except *Allah*, knows it all. Adopt your strategy based on local environment.

LESSONS FROM KASHMIR

I use the example of Shah Hamdan-Sufi from Central Asia, who came to Kashmir three times in 1372, 1378, and 1383, and with his influence there was mass conversion of the local population to Islam.

Converts predominantly were Hindus, and they used to sing songs in temple. To maintain a similar cultural practice, Shah Hamdan introduced *Avrad Fathi* after *Fajr* prayers – routine in Kashmir, recited loudly in rhythmic style after *Fajr* prayers and glorifies *Allah*. So, if a stranger walks by a mosque in Kashmir after *Fajr* prayers, they will hear "singing." This was the direct result of Shah Hamdan's adapting to the local culture and customs.

Many of the Hindus used to make sculptures and idols. Shah Hamdan introduced them to stone engravings, carpets, and handicrafts, which kept them busy with employment.

Because of the inclement climate in Kashmir, Shah Hamdan built Hamams which was used for communal baths. He used the time between Magrib and Isha for religious education *(Dawa)* – comfort and lectures.

Shah Hamdan's school of thought was different from the local one. He, Shah Hamdan, embraced the local one.

He brought with him over 700 scholars and established institutions of learning and *Dawa* throughout Kashmir.

Lessons: Think, adapt to local environment, be flexible, provide proper support and this will reinforce faith and *Dawa*.

MY SUGGESTIONS

PERSONAL APPROACH
Neighbors - interact with them and at work. Example of Prophet (PBUH): When asked to define a neighbor, he said 40 houses adjacent to you in all four directions. ICLI management has delivered a letter of greetings and thanks to 100-plus neighbors, along with a box of cookies. The response has been heartwarming.

1. One neighbor brought in a turkey as a gift.
2. Another one came personally to say thanks.
3. Many were thankful when the gift was delivered.
4. Mr. Joseph Jolly, 751 Franklin Street, Westbury, wrote, *Thanks for the cookies. It's been a pleasure having you and your congregation as a neighbor. All good things for you and your congregation in the New Year.*

MASS COMMUNICATIONS
Electronic media is now available. Use it. Send messages, responses, opinions.

OPINION MAKERS
News reporters - religious sections: Call them; invite them for unique

events - *Khatum Quran, Ameen, Eid* parties, marriages; introduce them to your rich heritage and culture.

ORGANIZATIONAL

ICLI: Interfaith - AMJID

December 5th Session: *Jerusalem* – Habeeb Ahmed informed the Muslims and non-Muslims as to the religious significance of Jerusalem. The next day, in *Newsday*, thousands learned from the report of this function and learned that the over-one-billion Muslims from around the world have a deep attachment towards the city of Jerusalem.

1. 1st *Qibla*
2. After Mecca, Medina the holiest city
3. Concept of *Isra/Miraj*

One Jewish participant commented - *We have to unlearn what was taught to us.*

DEMOGRAPHICS

The Muslim population in Nassau is spread out, to magnify impact; move adjacent to ICLI.

YOUTH

The role which our youth will play in accomplishing these goals is critical. A few remarks addressed to them –

The Muslim Student Association (MSA) chapters are growing at Stony Brook and other universities. The MSA leaders at Stony Brook and other colleges need to develop programs and products so as to explain Islam and Muslims to their co-students and faculty.

The youth at ICLI have organized a food drive. This is an example of faith in practice. Those who haven't done so, kindly contribute to this effort. We have engaged the young professionals and are working in developing programs with them. The youth here are in a unique position. Most of them have access to two sets of cultures – east and west from your parents. Take the best of both and develop a model from that.

ICLI has also been a supporter of the Muslim Student Network (MSN), which gives scholarships for college students for summer internship in Washington. It's a great experience. The future policymakers will, *Insha Allah*, develop from these activities.

Let me now highlight the contributions of some national organizations –MPAC: Muslim Public Affairs Council, and CAIR: Council on American Islamic Relations.

MPAC

At a recent presentation at the Suffolk Police Academy, I was asked, *Why are so many Muslims terrorists?* Thanks to MPAC work, I had access to the statistics for 1998. Attacks against US facilities and attacks in which US citizens suffered casualties totaled 111 – Eurasia 3, Africa 3, Western Europe 13, Middle East 5, and Latin America 87.

CAIR

In a recently concluded opinion poll by CAIR, I was pleased to note that over 96% of respondents felt Muslims should be actively engaged in local and national politics, and 56% had voted. In addition, a lot of other useful information was developed which will be of great help in the coming years.

(Washington, DC – 12/29/99) – CAIR asked media professionals to use one standard of newsworthiness when reporting on issues related to domestic and international terrorism. CAIR expressed concerns about an apparent imbalance in coverage whenever Muslims are involved, or alleged to be involved, in terrorist activities.

CAIR compared the coverage of three different news stories:

> 1.   The recent arrest of an Algerian man who allegedly tried to smuggle bomb-making materials into the United States.
>
> 2.   The arrest this month of two suspected militia members accused of plotting to blow up a California propane plant. (Officials say the resulting firestorm could have killed as many as half the people within a five-mile radius of the plant, and was intended to spark an uprising against the government.)
>
> 3.   The arrest on Tuesday of an American Airlines mechanic who was charged with possessing bomb-making materials after potential explosives and assault rifles were found in his home. White supremacist and anti-government publications were also found.

In the case of the Algerian suspect, a search of Lexis-Nexis and Dow Jones Interactive databases produced 129 (113 print, 16 broadcast) stories on the day of and the day following the announcement of the man's arrest. Twenty-one stories ran on page one.

The California propane plant case search produced 51 (51 print, 0 broadcast) stories on the day of the arrest and the following day. Only one of the stories ran on page one. Many of the stories ran as news briefs.

A similar search of stories related to the American Airlines mechanic produced a total of 10 articles. The New York Times ran the story on page 20. *The Washington Post* ran it on page 8. None of the propane plant or American Airlines stories highlighted the alleged perpetrator's race or religion.

According to a survey of national media outlets by the Muslim Internet news service, linkage of Islam and Muslims with terrorism has increased 51 percent since the beginning of the month of December.

The disparity in media coverage of terrorism-related stories involving Muslims is disturbing. Newsworthiness, not religion or ethnicity, should be the determining factor in the amount of coverage given to a particular story, said CAIR Board Chairman Omar Ahmad. Ahmad added that any Muslim who contemplates or carries out an act of violence in this country would face rejection and repudiation from the Islamic community.

AMERICAN MUSLIM ALLIANCE (AMA)
Grass-root mobilization and education of Muslims - Identify and encourage Muslims to run in elections. Morshad Alam, Senate NYS, was profiled in the December 28, 1999 issue of The New York Times, including quotation, *Politics is the same everywhere in the world. Nobody wants to give up their power. But times are changing* – Founder and President of the New American Democratic Club, Queens.

My recommendation is to support these and other organizations with your time and money. In conclusion, my message is that it's time for Muslims to think, reflect and act, and focus on issues which will give us an opportunity to interact with other faiths. Today's petition is an example of that effort.

We have over 40-million Americans who have no health insurance. This results in expensive and delayed care for these individuals. Two major organizations – Catholic Health Association of the USA with 2,000 members from the largest group of not-for-profit health-care sponsors, systems, facilities, health plans and related organizations. ACP-ASIM is a professional medical organization representing more than 115,000 doctors of Internal Medicine.

Lack of health insurance is a national tragedy, particularly in view of the economic prosperity. This must be addressed. Your name, city and Zip Code on the petition will be sent to the sponsors, and this will result in our participation in an issue which affects ALL of us, and thereby get connected with mainstream issues.

<table>
<tr><td>Rev. Michael D. Place</td><td>Dr. Whitney Addington</td></tr>
<tr><td>President and CEO</td><td>President, ACP-ASIM</td></tr>
<tr><td>The Catholic Health Association of USA</td><td>190 North Independence Mall West</td></tr>
<tr><td>1875 I Street NW, #1000</td><td>Philadelphia, PA 19106-1572</td></tr>
<tr><td>Washington, DC 20006-5409</td><td></td></tr>
</table>

Make Accessible and Affordable Health Care A National Policy

Dear Rev. Place and Dr. Addington:

Thank you for initiating a discussion on health-care reform. We are in total agreement with you in that the lack of adequate health coverage for a very large segment of Americans is intolerable, particularly in view of the economic prosperity that exists in the USA. We also agree that the lack of health insurance in the long run costs more and leads to inadequate care of the uninsured, particularly from the minority groups, women and children.

We applaud and support the joint initiative of the Catholic Health Association and the American College of Physicians-American Society of Internal Medicine (ACP-ASIM) and are delighted to add our support to this initiative.

Sincerely,

In conclusion, we are mindful of the past but we should be focused on the future, and to quote Murad Hoffman, *It is not far-fetched to expect the intellectual and spiritual revivification of Islam in the 21st century to be kindled and propelled from research done by qualified Muslim thinkers working outside dar al Islam.* Fellow Muslims, Murad Hoffman is referring to you.

I leave you with 4 C's, 4 P's, and 3 A's.

De-emphasize: Accent, Appearance, Ancestry.

Emphasize: Courage, Competence, Character, Clarity.

Use: your Pen, Phone – this will result in Power, Politics.

Chapter 11

<u>THREE UNIQUE EVENTS</u>

There are three very special events held at ICLI that have left an indelible mark on me, and I would share these with the readers:

1. The Visit of Dr. Robert Pinckney, Superintendent, Westbury School District, and Resulting Development of Mentorship Program.

2. Terry Anderson's Visit - What does a former hostage in Lebanon have to say about his "Muslim" captors?

3. Roy Gutman's Visit - Irish-Catholic Congressman Awarding, on Behalf of ICLI, an American Jew Whose Reporting Saved Thousands of Bosnian Muslims - Only in America.

> *Quran* Chapter 96 Verses 1-5
> *1. Proclaim! (or Read!)*
> *In the name*
> *Of thy Lord and Cherisher,*
> *Who created -*
>
> *2. Created man, out of*
> *A (mere) clot*
> *Of congealed blood:*
>
> *3. Proclaim! And thy Lord*
> *Is Most Bountiful -*
>
> *4. He Who taught*
> *(The use of) the Pen -*
>
> *5. Taught man that*
> *Which he knew not.*

The *Quranic* instruction of the importance of reading and writing was the <u>first</u> revelation to Prophet Muhammad (PBUH). Muslims, therefore, are encouraged to pursue education and acquire new skills. A famous saying of the Prophet was, *Seek knowledge, even if you have to go to China to do this.*

110

DR. ROBERT D. PINCKNEY SPEAKS AT ISLAMIC CENTER

ICLI, as a community, has pursued education with vigor, purpose and vitality. This is done for children and adults and is not just restricted to members of ICLI. It was in this spirit that Dr. Robert D. Pinckney, Superintendent of Westbury School District, was invited to ICLI to share his views regarding education in public schools, and how a community such as ICLI could contribute in helping to upgrade and improve standards. Excerpts from Dr. Pinckney's presentation as reported in the *Westbury Times* of March 16, 1995 are reproduced below.

Dr. Pinckney Speaks at Islamic Center
Unveils New Educational Initiatives
By Danny McCue
The Westbury Times, March 16, 1995

Dr. Robert D. Pinckney, Superintendent of Schools for the Westbury School District, stood before a crowded room at the Islamic Center of Long Island and said that he and every other person in attendance must strive to "change the norm" if Westbury and the nation's schools are to be a success in the 21st century.

Dr. Pinckney's much-anticipated appearance at the Center, co-sponsored by LIFE (Learning Is For Everyone), the Central Westbury Civic Association, and the NAACP drew nearly 100 people, including residents of Westbury and New Cassel, as well as members of the Islamic Center itself.

The superintendent said he had come to the Center because he wanted to reach out to professionals in the community and get them involved in enhancing the curriculum of the schools. The vast majority of Muslims who worship at the Center and see it as their spiritual focal point fit that bill, being highly regarded in the fields of medicine and finance.

Dr. Pinckney then unveiled three programs that will be kicked off at the start of the next school year with the assistance of the Islamic Center. The first is called "career explorations expectations" and is aimed at giving local students real perspective on the kinds of opportunities that will exist for them in the working world after graduation.

111

If all goes according to plan, fifth, sixth and seventh graders attending Westbury schools will even be afforded the chance to "shadow" various professionals on a one-to-one, day-to-day basis to get a vivid taste of the world outside of the classrooms.

Along the same lines, Dr. Pinckney is working with the Center to develop an apprenticeship/internship program for the district's seniors. He hopes to expand the professions the internship program would cover as more local professionals come forward get involved.

Lastly, beginning in September of next year, Dr. Pinckney plans to establish a workshop schedule covering topics of vital concern to today's teens. These workshops would be held at the Islamic Center and in the district's own facilities and cover everything from stopping smoking (Westbury will be a smoke-free district as of the first day of classes next year.) to teen pregnancy.

In reaching out to the professionals in attendance, Dr. Pinckney said he was asking them "to make an investment in the future of your community and your country."

"I feel that children should be educated regardless of where they come from, and what they bring to the school house door," he said. "I'm asking you to support the children of Westbury's public schools and to do so in a way that demonstrates something to them and has the added benefit of helping them to feel good about themselves."

As is often his way, Dr. Pinckney used a mixture of humor, cold hard facts, and the gift of a story teller to illustrate for his listeners exactly what his district - and all districts - are up against in terms of raising academic standards.

"I once heard a basketball coach bemoaning the performance of his team by saying something like, "And we spent three hours practicing the night before."

"And I thought to myself, did they also spend three hours doing math, or science?" Dr. Pinckney continued, "In all probability, many parents accompanied their children to that practice and stayed for

112

all three hours. I wonder when was the last time they took their children to the library and sat there with them for three hours.

"We have to instill a love of learning early in life, otherwise we wind up with a situation that is all too common today: students who are embarrassed by success."

To illustrate his point, he recalled a young woman who scored a 96 on a test, but claimed she only got a 60 when he asked how well she had done.

"Even then," Dr. Pinckney recalled, "she would only say "60" as a whisper. Meanwhile there was one student who got a 15 on the same test - and he was telling everyone about it.

"Another time I discovered that I had a bright young man in my midst who wanted to do well but wouldn't carry his books home to study.

"I'm ashamed to walk home with books," he said. "If I do I'll be ostracized by my boys," Dr. Pinckney said.

"Now I solved it by getting him two sets of books," the superintendent continued. "But the problem for me was, why couldn't he carry his books home?

"Children have innate wisdom, regardless of their native tongue and where they come from. Our job is to change the negative notion. We've got to work against the notion that it's not fashionable to be smart.

"Many of our students are getting caught up in images and appearances, not the things that will last forever,"Dr. Pinckney said.

"What we need to strive for and what I believe we're reaching for in initiating programs such as those discussed today is a world where young people can say, "Dad, Mom, it's fun to be smart."

All the suggestions made by Dr. Pinckney were adapted and followed up. We have summarized the results of the hospital-school program elsewhere. (Chapter 5)

ISLAM, TOLERANCE AND TERRORISM

TERRY ANDERSON VISITS ICLI - DECEMBER 15, 1996

In September 1996 former hostage Terry Anderson gave a speech titled *Islam, Tolerance and Terrorism* at a Unitarian Church in Shelter

Rock, Long Island. Members of ICLI, in particular Al Haaj Ghazi Khankan who attended this meeting, extended an invitation to Mr. Anderson to visit ICLI, and for the first time Mr. Anderson spoke to a group of about 100 Muslims in a mosque. Mr. Anderson's visit was extremely beneficial, and we reproduce some of his remarks as reported in *Newsday* on December 16, 1996 and the *Westbury Times* on December 26, 1996.

From Terror to Tolerance
Anderson Speaks at Mosque
Newsday

Yesterday morning was the first time Anderson spoke at a mosque. He addressed about 100 Muslims.

Accompanied by his Lebanese wife, Madeline Bassil Anderson, Anderson spoke of understanding and forgiveness. He stressed the need for Americans to understand Muslims and the conflicts of the Middle East as the Muslim community grows in the United States. Long Island has 12 Islamic centers and about 30,000 Muslims.

"I'm not trying to teach these people anything,"Anderson said before his speech as he smoked a cigarette outside in the cool morning air.

"I want to talk about the American perception of Islam. Americans have a simplistic view of Muslims. On the whole, they see them as Arab. They tend to see them as fundamentalist, and they tend to see them as violent. We know that picture is . . . . inaccurate.

"I've had experience . . . . I know there are lots of different kinds of Muslims with different interpretations of the one belief."

Abdulah Karcic, 66, of East Meadow, a Bosnian Muslim, said his people "suffered from Christians who held Bibles under their arms while they executed Muslims." Karcic said he could not "identify what they (Christians) do with the religion or the teachings of the religion."

Anderson, the Associated Press' chief Middle East correspondent when he was kidnapped in 1985 by the Hezbollah party, had time to ponder religious, political and economic reasons that motivated his captors.

114

"After a while, you develop a relationship," he said. "We all had lots of time. I was chained to the wall. I attempted to understand them."

Among his hard-won discoveries, Anderson said, is that Islam teaches tolerance rather than violence; Islam is interpreted in different ways by different people; and that Americans need to know the difference between Islam and political extremists who use the religion as a guise for their violence.

"My captors, who were violent, never attemped to convert me or prevent me from practicing my own religion," said Anderson, who is Roman Catholic. "The first thing . . . . they granted me was a Bible."

"We are going to have to deal with Islam and fundamentalism forever. We have to understand them. We don't have to agree with them, but for our own self-interest, we need to . . . . listen to them."

Faces of Faith
Former Hostage Sees Many Sides to Muslims
By Daniel J. McCue
Westbury Times - December 26, 1996

During his six-and-a-half years as a hostage of political extremists in Lebanon, former Associated Press Bureau Chief Terry Anderson had a considerable amount of time to contemplate his captors.

"After all, I was chained to the wall and wasn't going anywhere," he said last Sunday as he addressed more than 100 members of the Islamic Center of Long Island in Westbury.

Since his release, what he has mostly attempted to do is comprehend the contradiction between his captors' strong religious beliefs and their actions.

"In many respects, Islam as a religion is far more tolerant of differing views than other faiths," he said. "For instance, the Koran teaches respect for 'people of the 'Book,' Christians and Jews."

"Interestingly, my captors, who were violent men, never tried to convert me to Islam, nor did they ever interfere with my practice of religion." Mr. Anderson, a Catholic, continued, "In fact, the first thing I asked them for and the first thing they grant-

115

ed me was the Bible."

That Bible, an American standard Bible, which his captors bought brand new from a shop near to where he was being held, remained with Mr. Anderson throughout his ordeal and he said, "It was lying beside my cot the day I left."

"My guard sees me everyday. He does not appear insane. He knows I did him no harm. I see little in him that I do not recognize."

The Islamic Center of Long Island is the first mosque Terry Anderson has ever spoken in, and the invitation to do so came as something of a surprise to both the speaker and the man who extended it.

"You know because you live here that most Americans have a very simplistic and sadly inaccurate view of Islam and Muslims," Mr. Anderson said after he stepped to the podium.

"If you ask most Americans what a Muslim is, they first say, 'an Arab.' Secondly, they say, 'fundamentalist.' And thirdly, and most sadly, they say, 'violent.'

"Those three things go together in the American consciousness, and the reason is what they've seen on television and read in the newspapers.

Recalling His Captors

"Yes, I've had experience with that kind of Islam," Mr. Anderson said, making reference to his fundamentalist captors. "But I've also experienced many others. There are more than five million Muslims in the United States - there are more Muslims here than Episcopalians."

Mr. Anderson was kidnapped by members of the radical Hezbollah party as he walked along a Beirut street in 1985, and through six-and-a-half years as a hostage and in the five years since his release what he has mostly attempted to do is comprehend the contradiction between his captors' strong religious beliefs and their actions.

"In many respects, Islam as a religion is far more tolerant of differing views than other faiths," he said. For instance, the Koran teaches respect for the 'people of the book,' Christians and Jews.

"Yes, there are Muslims who are terrorists," the former reporter told an audience conditioned to flinch at the intermingling of the two phrases, "but I have never attempted to say that they represent all Muslims. They don't. They don't even represent all fundamentalists. Fundamentalism in Islam, to my understanding, is not an advocacy of violence. Yet Americans see that. They don't understand the diversity of believers in your faith."

Though conceding that he is not an Islamic scholar, Mr. Anderson said he has read the Islamic Bible, the Holy Koran, and many other works on the faith, and has found "nothing that promotes violence."

"There is nothing in the words of the Prophet (Mohammed) that promotes intolerance and violence. In fact, the instruction of the Koran, to me, is to love God and live in conformity with others. That's why I still have many questions about Islam."

Mr. Anderson characterized the men who held him as "religious men who understand the Koran in an enormously different way than most Muslims do."

"It has to do with politics, power, and economics, but not very much with the actual practice of religion," he explained. "It's that way with many groups in many faiths who attempt to describe themselves and their actions as those of 'true believers.'"

And yet, Mr. Anderson admitted, it was hard to come to terms with his captors' religiousness in light of his predicament.

"I could never understand how they could claim to believe in Islam, kneel five times a day next to me, praying in the name of Allah the compassionate, and Allah the merciful, and yet kidnap people and kill people. How do you reconcile that?"

"To my mind we cannot separate the things we do from what we are. It is said in Christianity that we should hate the sin, but love the sinner, but I will never love those who held me. I am not Christ. But I will try to forgive."

117

A Dialogue Develops

If Mr. Anderson could, he said, one thing he would like to do is take from the American mind the image of Muslims as bearded, violent men. That isn't any more valid an image than saying all Catholics are violent because of incidents in Northern Ireland.

"My hope is that what you are doing here and my speaking here will contribute to that understanding," he said.

To illustrate his point about what must change in some sectors of contemporary Islamic society, Mr. Anderson spoke of a tape his guards listened to constantly. "All it contained was those very repetitive chants, and they listened to it hour after hour after hour. It would drive us crazy.

"Finally, I asked one of the more intelligent of my guards, "Why are you doing this? It doesn't say anything. It's not teaching you anything.

"He responded by saying, 'Because it stops me from thinking.'

"This strain of 'You shouldn't think for yourself; I'll tell you what to think' is not Islamic, it is not an Islamic teaching, and yet, from experience, I can tell you that it is present in many Islamic countries."

There followed a long and animated discussion of terrorism, during which several audience members said what Westerners see as terrorism is actually a 'reaction to the greater terrorism, the world order' in the words of one man.

"Big powers oppress smaller powers. Islam as a religion does not endorse any kind of terrorism, but it does give us the right to defend ourselves."

"Intellectually, I understand what you are saying, but personally, I don't care what the greater terrorism is," Mr. Anderson said. "I don't care what society is doing to you. Taking an innocent hostage or an innocent life is wrong. I cannot accept it and I will not justify it anymore than I will justify an abused young man growing up in poverty going out and killing somebody. What we're talking about is a personal, human choice.

"International society and world economics don't dictate your personal actions; you do," he said.

A Question Not Answered

During the filming of the CNN documentary, the title of which is adapted from Mr. Anderson's book about his experiences as a prisoner, the former journalist asked the secretary general if he would admit that his kidnapping was wrong or a mistake.

"I can't say that," the secretary general replied.

"Do you know how hard it is for me to understand that?" Mr. Anderson said, still visibly aghast. "It's five years later. This is a man who reads, who is educated. I just cannot understand that."

Mr. Anderson also asked the leader of the Hezbollah whether he could envision any circumstances, any circumstances at all, in which he could live at peace with Israel.

"His answer, briefly, was, 'No.'"

Many in attendance at the mosque heartily and very vocally agreed.

Mr. Khankan offered a spirited defense of the Hezbollah position, saying that while Islam teaches tolerance, and while it is, in fact, an easy thing to co-exist with both Christians and Jews, a great many Muslims see Israel as an oppressive state.

"The British and the French occupied many of our territories and left. We see Israel as a similar occupying force," Mr. Khankan said.

Mr. Anderson recalled a prayer his mother taught him.

"Lord, give me the power to change the things that I can change, the calmness to accept the things I cannot, and the wisdom to know the difference . . . .

"I have to tell you, Israel is not going away. You have to understand that," he continued.

He then offered them some personal advice.

"You are all American citizens now. You have the right to organize, to lobby, and to vote. If you really want America to adopt a more neutral position in terms of Middle Eastern affairs, work at it, but realize that you have to do it in a way Americans can understand.

"That means you are going to have to deal with some things. You're going to have to give me answers that are different from the ones you are giving me today. You're going to have to get off the train you're on and say that if Israel becomes a place of justice, a place where no one is treated unfairly, then, yes, you can accept its existence.

"And remember, while unfortunate things do sometimes happen in Israel, unfortunate things happened at the start of every new, independent country. More than anything, you have to say, no matter what the oppression, we reject the response to it that I've experienced.

"If you truly want to change the course of U.S. foreign policy, then you have to present your opinion in a way that Americans can understand.

"I have been a journalist for most of my life, and I've seen a lot of obstacles to getting to the truth. I've seen a lot of spinning of the facts being done over the years. Yet I firmly believe that the truth does come out. I really do believe that truth and justice do express themselves eventually," Mr. Anderson said.

Afterwards, many members of the Islamic Center applauded Mr. Anderson for his presentation and his frankness.

"He's learning. We're learning. We're all learning together," one woman said. "That's the way it should be."

"I was very impressed with his demeanor, his positive outlook, and his attempt to understand the reasons behind his unfortunate imprisonment," Dr. Faroque Khan, a member of the Center's board of directors said later.

"I think he did a good job of separating the tenets of religion from the intricacies of politics, and that he's got a good feel for the issues confronting the Muslim community.

"I was very impressed with him . . . .if I went through what he went through, I don't know how I would have come out," Dr. Khan said.

A TRIBUTE TO ROY GUTMAN FOR HIS REPORTING OF THE BOSNIA GENOCIDE

During the past century Europe has witnessed brutalities and killings on an unparalleled scale. The holocaust perpetuated in Nazi Germany in the 40's is well known and recorded. Millions of individuals were killed simply because of their religion. We had heard the slogan *Never again* over and over again.

Unfortunately, in the 90's we once again witnessed mass killings of large numbers of Europeans simply because they professed being Muslims. The genocide committed against Bosnian Muslims left thousands dead and many more homeless and as refugees.

During the genocide in Bosnia, a reporter from *Newsday*, Roy W. Gutman, stood out for his outstanding journalistic integrity and reporting. Thanks to his reporting the *concentration camps* were identified, an international spotlight was put on them, and thousands of imprisoned Muslims were saved. ICLI recognized this and a special event in honor of Roy W. Gutman was held on Saturday, February 20, 1999.

Mr. Gutman's journalistic contributions had received recognition from various groups, including the prestigious *Pulitzer Award* for his coverage of Bosnia. Mr. Gutman, a *Newsday* reporter since 1982, is a former National Security reporter and served as a European Bureau Chief from 1989 to 1994. He currently covers issues and institutions of international security in Washington, DC. He is a recipient of the *Pulitzer Prize for International Reporting* for his Bosnia coverage, the *Polk Award for Best Foreign Reporting, the Selden Ring Award for Investigative Reporting,* the *National Headliner Award for Best-of-Show Prize, the New York Deadline Club Investigative Reporting Prize, the Heywood Brown Award of the Newpaper Guild,* and the *Hal Boyle Award of the Overseas Press Club.* In 1992, he also earned the *Special Human Rights in Media Award of the International League for Human Rights* for his reporting on Serb atrocities in Bosnia, and the *Newsday Publisher's Award for Exceptional Achievement.* Mr. Gutman was previously employed by Reuters News Agency for 11 years. He has served as Bureau Chief for Yugoslavia, State Department correspondent, and chief Capital Hill reporter. Mr. Gutman has multiple publications to his credit; he is fluent in German and has conversational ability in Serbo-Croatian.

During this event, Mr. Gutman heard a firsthand account from the Karcic family – Abdullah, Emina and their son, Dr. Arsad Karcic – who told Mr. Gutman that they are alive simply because of his reporting. This was one of the most moving and emotional evenings, and there was a sense of immense gratitude and thanks for Mr. Gutman. He was accompanied by his wife and daughter. Mr. Robert Keeler, another *Newsday Pulitzer* awardee, commented on how he felt proud of being a journalist because of the type of work his colleague Roy Gutman had done.

Mr. Gutman, in his remarks, commented on this remarkable evening and how he felt proud and privileged to meet people, face to face, who had benefited from his efforts.

Congressman Peter King, in his comments summed up the spirit of the evening by stating, "Only in American will you have an Irish Catholic give an award to an American Jew on behalf of American Muslims."

Mr. Gene Turner, Congressman King's Chief of Staff, stated, "We need to learn to host these types of events." From my perspective, we were simply saying thank you to someone who had done something to correct an injustice.

Chapter 12

WHAT OTHERS HAVE TO SAY ABOUT ICLI

OUR NEIGHBORS:
RUDOLPH H. CLARK, Ph.D.

Dr. Rudolph H. Clark has had immense experience in the area of human resource development in both private and public sectors. He is President of R.H. Clark & Associates, an African-American-owned, multi-ethnic, private research organization. A long-time resident of Westbury and a former President of the Westbury School Board, Dr. Clark was directly responsible for hiring the first two African-American principals, the first African-American Superintendent, and numerous African-American teachers. He is President of the Westbury NAACP with the largest membership in the history of Long Island.

In many ways the Islamic Center of Long Island has been the most impacting experience to occur in the Westbury/New Cassel community in the last thirty years. As an impressionable adolescent in Harlem, I was superficially exposed to the Black Muslim movement on the Honorable Elijah Mohammed. However, this represented too much of a cultural and religious shock to my traditional Catholic background and training. My interest and awareness of the Islamic religion was further stimulated when I worked in Nigeria and had an opportunity to meet and know many Moslems. The ICLI again gave me an opportunity to broaden my consciousness and presented the challenge to focus on a different religious orientation. Initially, when I think about the ICLI, the incredibly beautiful mosque and its "strangeness" in what appears to be an alien ambience stimulate me. I am literally overcome by a "rush" of curiosity to learn more about this different and appealing place.

There are numerous features offered by the ICLI that should be adapted by other centers, churches and places of worship. Paramount among these activities is your Community Outreach programs and your efforts to build coalitions with other faiths and/or organizations. The ICLI is indeed a reservoir of information and challenges. My experiences at ICLI have been warm, enriching and stimulating.

KENNETH AND MILDRED LITTLE
Kenneth and Mildred Little, residents of the New Cassel community for 40 years, have been active since PTA, Drum & Bugle, Boy Scouts, Youth Center, Community Center, Kiwanis, Health Center, Town of North

Hempstead Master Plan, Community Development, Board of Zoning and Appeals, numerous committees and activities, Co-Presidents of Progressive Civic Association of New Cassel, Inc., and presently New Cassel Environmental Justice Project, Inc.

During our years of civic association workings to improve the quality of life in the New Cassel community, we have encountered many problems and have tried to solve most.

Several years ago residents observed many cars in front of their homes and wondered where are they going. Suddenly we discover a mosque on the avenue, but the building is in the Village of Westbury – why are the cars over here? Are "they" moving in? Then we remember we were "they" not too long ago.

Various civic and community members met with members of the Board of Trustees, Dr. Khan and Ghazi Khankan to discuss the community's concerns as to the problem. This meeting of dialogue from both sides gave all an education and brought about a solution. A working relationship was developed on working together for the good of all.

We attended many meetings of government officials, professional members and community residents that were learning experiences to all. A meeting with Dr. Bernard Harris, the first African-American space astronaut, was truly an experience.

The community has worked with members of the Center on many activities for the community. Ghazi Khankan worked diligently with members of the community to establish the New Cassel Environmental Justice Project, Inc., attending endless meetings and meeting with elected officials in our quest for funding. Mohammed Ahmed is a board member and treasurer of the New Cassel Environmental Justice Project, Inc.

The Islamic Center of Long Island is a perfect example of how all can come together and work toward the goals of all. A wider range of publicity about the workings and events of the Center will bring about an understanding to all.

ROBERT D. PINCKNEY, Ph.D.

Dr. Robert Pinckney is a native Long Islander. After high school, Dr. Pinckney attended and graduated from Delaware State University with a BS degree. He earned a Masters Degree from Adelphi University, his Professional Diploma in Educational Administration from Long Island University, and a Ph.D. from Iowa State University.

Dr. Pinckney has served as a teacher, coach, advisor and building administrator in various school organizations on Long Island and Maryland. He has also served as the Assistant Superintendent for the Freeport Public Schools, as well as Superintendent of the Westbury Public School, before his retirement in August 1999.

The Islamic Center of Long Island (ICLI) presence in the Long Island community serves as a symbolic and cultural statement for all.

It symbolizes the commitment of a group of people, from different parts of the world, who wanted to practice and share their cultural and religious beliefs. The center's edifice makes this statement real everyday. Every effort is made to bring speakers into the community to provide current points of view on matters of health, education, politics and social relevance.

During my visit, I felt a personal elation to see the commitment to education and family. I saw numbers of children of various ages and their families going about their activities in an atmosphere of love and support. This level of nurturing is key to today's youth.

Without a doubt, the ICLI has and will continue to be a positive force in the religious and political community on Long Island for time to come.

MANNIE AND ANN SWEAT

Mr. Mannie Sweat is President of the Central Westbury Civic Association, and Ms. Ann Sweat is a member of various community organizations. The Sweats represent a "dream couple." They are life-long residents of Westbury and are deeply involved in the civic and educational activities of the community. The Sweats are frequent visitors and participants at ICLI and have helped ICLI launch several initiatives with a goal of upgrading the quality of life in Westbury/Nassau.

The Village of Westbury is a community of growing cultural diversity. The many houses of worship bring a special mightiness to help make the community strong, safe and spiritually healthy.

The Islamic Center of Long Island is located in the Village of Westbury. We, Mannie and Ann Sweat, life-long residents of Westbury, took pride in assisting the ICLI come to life in its embryonic stages. Our thoughts were shared in a New York Times article which were met with pro's and con's by the community.

We worked with the ICLI continually since 1991 and more specifically with Dr. Faroque Khan. The magnetic relationship has born fruit and given birth and rise to a few project we would like to share:

1991:   Working with the Westbury Building Department; Michelle Depew, Superintendent, Building Department, to assist in securing the Certificate of Occupancy for the Islamic Center of Long Island.

1994:   *Being invited by Dr. Faroque Khan as his guests to attend the Annual ICLI celebration.*

1996:   *Highlights: Worked with Dr. Faroque Khan, Chair of Medical Department, Nassau County Medical Center, and Dr. Robert Pinckney, Superintendent, Westbury Public Schools, at a Central Westbury Civic Association meeting to establish an internship program in the Department of Medicine at the Nassau County Medical Center. This internship was the first of its kind, opening the doors for minority students to get exposure to seek careers in the medical profession.*

1997:   *Dr. Faroque Khan arranged for Dr. Bernard Harris, the first African-American astronaut-physician to go to the outer space in a space vehicle, to visit the Westbury Public Schools and share with the students his space adventure.*

1997:   *At present, we are working with Dr. Khan on various health committees throughout Nassau County, addressing health concerns and issues as it pertains to the minority community.*

1998:   *We attend lectures given at the ICLI where prominent scholars speak. We were particularly thrilled to meet Terry Anderson where he signed his book and spoke for hours regarding his Lebanon experience.*

2000:   *Continuation of many past and new projects.*

We salute you, Dr. Faroque Khan, and prayerfully look forward to many years of commitment and giving each other of the blessings we have so bountifully received for the betterment of our fellow man and community in which we live.

PUBLIC OFFICIALS

MATTHEW A. CUOMO

Mr. Matthew A. Cuomo is a practicing attorney and a political activist in the Democratic Party in Nassau County. He was a candidate for the Nassau Legislative election in 1999.

I was invited to appear at the ICLI during Nassau County's Legislative election season in 1999. Running as a Democrat in a heavily Republican District, I had come to understand it was not important that people pledge their support to me before I had said anything, but that people were willing to listen and discuss the issues before making a decision. When I

spoke at the ICLI, that is exactly what happened. I was given the oppor-
tunity to present my ideas and then those ideas were discussed. Looking
back, whether I convinced all those in attendance that my ideas were cor-
rect and that they should vote for me was not most important. Most sig-
nificant about the experience was the fostering of our Democratic system
through a lively exchange of ideas.

As I walked through the center and was introduced to various members by
my host, Dr. Khan, it became very clear to me that the ICLI was much more
than a place of worship. It was and is a facility that serves the broader
aspects of the community. Most importantly, being a non-Muslim, I was
made to feel welcome. The ICLI has taken the best of religion and commu-
nity and combined them to serve its members and the community as a whole.

THOMAS P. DI NAPOLI
Mr. Thomas P. DiNapoli was elected to represent the 16th District of
Nassau County in the Assembly of the State of New York. He is
ex-Chairman of the Nassau County Democratic Committee and is a candidate for the County Executive position in 2001..

I recall my visit to your mosque with great appreciation for the hospital-
ity extended to me. My most vivid and lasting impression is of the warmth
and generosity of all who greeted me at the Islamic Center of Long Island.
I was made to feel totally welcome in your house of worship as a valued
guest. The care and attention you and your colleagues extended to me
helped me to better understand the many dimensions of the Islamic tradi-
tion and served as a wonderful introduction to your faith.

Besides being struck by the friendliness of the congregation, I was struck
by the diversity of the countries represented in your membership. Muslim
families, originating from around the world and now residing on Long
Island, have found a home at the Islamic Center of Long Island.

The simplicity of the beauty of the building was appealing to me. You
have constructed a magnificent facility in which to worship, contemplate,
and pray. Given the phenomenal growth in your membership since the
opening of the Center in 1984, it is clear that our Muslim community is
being very well served.

The congregation of the Islamic Center of Long Island is full of faith,
energy, intelligence, and compassion. I thank you for your on-going serv-
ice to our community.

DONNA FERRARA

Ms. Donna Ferrara was elected to represent the 15th Assembly District in 1992. She is currently the ranking Republican member on the Insurance Committee, the Vice Chair of the Minority Program Committee, and a member of the Tourism, Ethics and Guidance, and Consumer Affairs Committees. Ms. Ferrara is married to Robert Gregory and they have a one-year-old daughter, Kathleen Lillian.

I have been to ICLI on several occasions and I have always received a warm and gracious welcome. The many educational programs that are provided by ICLI come to mind when I think about the Center. These programs provide an excellent service to the community. I am pleased to have ICLI in my Assembly District and proud of the benefits this organization brings to our community. I hope the mosque will remain a part of the district, continue with its excellent traditions and grow into a long-standing pillar for our community.

THOMAS G. GULOTTA

Mr. Thomas G. Gulotta has been the County Executive of Nassau County for over 12 years. He has visited ICLI several times and has engaged the Muslim community actively in the public arena. Al Haaj Ghazi Khankan, a member of ICLI, was appointed a liaison for the Muslim community by Mr. Gulotta.

America is a melting pot of nationalities and heritages. It is a land where people from all backgrounds strive to co-exist in an atmosphere of mutual respect and support.

The Islamic Center of Long Island has made a significant effort to promote an environment of human compassion and mutual respect in which our residents can live, work and raise a family.

The Center is also recognized as a prominent contributor to community life, support various religious, cultural, educational and humanitarian concerns. Today, as in the past, the Center affords worshippers and visitors alike the opportunity to share in the enriched appreciation of Muslim heritage and tradition.

On behalf of the citizens of Nassau County, I commend and thank the Islamic Center of Long Island for its outstanding efforts to enhance the quality of life in Nassau County. I thank you for caring enough to make a difference.

PETER T. KING

Congressman Peter T. King has represented the Third Congressional

District since 1992. He has visited ICLI several times, shared his political insight with the group, presided over special events such as the recognition of Roy Gutman – *Newsday* reporter – and, more recently, held a book-reading session at one of the Sunday morning adult sessions where he read his book "Terrible Beauty." One of the ICLI students, Sami Mir, did a summer internship in Congressman King's office in 1999.

Long before I ever set foot inside a mosque, I was heavily involved in a high-profile congressional debate defending the human rights of Muslims, especially in Bosnia, Kosova and Kashmir. I believe that's the reason I was first invited to visit the Islamic Center of Long Island.

That first encounter was very memorable. I couldn't help but be impressed with the work ethic, devotion to family and spiritual commitment so evident at the Center.

It has been gratifying for me to help build a political awareness in this, the fastest growing religious group in America.

GENE TURNER

Mr. Gene Turner is a former newspaper reporter who spent 30 years in federal and local government – and politics – until his retirement in the middle of 1999. He served as press secretary to County Executives Ralph Caso and Francis Purcell and as executive assistant to successive supervisors in the Town of Hempstead: Thomas Gulotta, Joseph Mondello and Gregory Peterson.

In the U.S. House of Representatives, Mr. Turner completed a term as minority staff director of a congressional subcommittee in Washington, D.C. before returning to his home base of Long Island to act as District Director for the office of former Congressman Norman Lent.

Immediately prior to his recent retirement Mr. Turner was District Administrator in the Long Island office of Congressman Peter T. King.

The Islamic Center of Long Island, whose architectural design combines the modern and the traditional, seems to me to be representative of the Muslim community it serves. Mothers in traditional garb supervise happy children in western wear – jeans and sneakers.

But on a somewhat higher level, I see a thriving community zealously protecting its traditional values while assimilating, with astonishing success, into Long Island society, its neighborhoods, its professions, and its academic institutions.

I have been proud to play a small part in assisting those in the Muslim community who wish to take their place in the sometimes Byzantine Long Island political system. Working with Dr. Faroque Khan, among others, I have had the privilege to share my experiences during 30 years of local political involvement and to offer some advice to those eager to participate.

Locally and nationally, the political environment can only be improved by the entry of individuals whose religious convictions commit them to integrity and hard work in pursuit of a better life for all, regardless of religion, race or ethnic background.

SOME PROMINENT VISITORS TO ICLI

FEISAL ABDUL-RAUF

Mr. Feisal Abdul-Rauf was born in Kuwait and educated in Egypt, England, Malaysia and the United States. He is the Imam of the Farah Mosque in New York City, and is a prolific writer and lecturer on Islam.

As I see it, because the ICLI was founded by some of the most highly successful Muslims within the community, it has not only filled the immediate needs of a place for prayer and Sunday-school education for the children, but also has seen itself as part of the overall American community. Thus, through its interfaith programs, networking with the press and political activity, it has made the Muslim community's voice heard and respected.

The adult education programs are another praiseworthy feature that has contributed to the continual expansion of the minds and attitudes of Muslims, and increased their awareness of issues that they ought to think about, whether as responsible parents, as civic-minded people within the community, whether Muslim or not.

The Center has also enhanced the respect of the non-Muslim community towards Islam and its cultural, artistic and intellectual heritage. Without the Center, there is no doubt in my mind that Islam and Muslims would have had less positive exposure.

NIHAD AWAD

Ms. Nihad Awad is the Executive Director of the Council of American Islamic Relations.

The weekly ICLI faxes which we receive at CAIR serve as reminders that ICLI is one of the best organized and most effective Islamic centers in the nation.

In 1996 I had the pleasure of visiting ICLI to organize a local response to the Anti-Terrorism Bill and the unconstitutional use of secret evidence against Muslims and Arabs. About 40 people attended the seminar. I asked the participants to write letters to their members of Congress to urge them to vote against the use of secret evidence. Seven minutes later I walked out of that meeting with 37 letters.

Another thing that made an impression on me was the way the leadership at ICLI make full use of the community power gathered at Juma'a prayer. Outside the main door long brown tables were lined up with petitions taped on them. People were stopping to sign the petitions one after another with the pens provided on the tables. In minutes, hundreds of people had empowered the mosque to express their solid stand on issues of the day.

RABBI KAREN BENDER

Rabbi Karen Bender is a frequent visitor to the Islamic Center of Long Island and a participant of American Muslims and Jews in Dialogue (AMJID).

The Islamic Center of Long Island is a community center and house of worship which is vital to the religious vibrancy of Long Island. The lay people there are true leaders and educators and they are courageous when it comes to building bridges with other communities on Long Island.

As Jews, we feel fortunate to have partners for unity, diversity and friendship in the Islamic Center of Long Island. To those of us at Temple Beth-El of Great Neck, the membership of Islamic Center of Long Island constitute family as much as friends.

MS. ROHANA FILIPPI

Ms. Rohana Filippi was born and raised in Italy, and educated in art through the inheritance of Italy's fine tradition. She traveled extensively. Since the late 1960's Ms. Filippi developed her own style of Arabic script. Her art is entirely devoted to the expression of *Allah's* presence everywhere.

Though she is now a Muslim, Ms. Filippi grew up Catholic in a decidedly non-Arabic environment. She graduated in philosophy and pedagogy and learned to speak fluently Italian, French, Spanish and English.

Currently Ms. Filippi lives in Manhattan. In addition to her artistic work, she represents a non-governmental organization to the UN and promotes its social humanitarian projects.

ICLI is a very friendly and warm Center where I was welcomed from the very first time I was introduced to the community as an Islamic artist. It's

131

a place where people are kind and committed, and that's why I would like to be able to spend more time there (I live in Manhattan), and share more of the activities that are scheduled along the year. The Masjid of the Long Island Islamic Center is, in itself, a building full of light and open space, which somehow reflects the philosophy of the people in charge of organizing the programs for the community.

I particularly appreciate lectures and meetings that help to develop an open-mind and interfaith attitude among the audience, as well as conferences on Islamic topics. In my opinion, we all need to develop a wider and more tolerant approach to the diversity of mankind and I'm glad to see that happening at ICLI. Insh'Allah other centers in the USA will adopt this policy.

Another thing that I like a lot at ICLI is the "pace" of prayers. Everyone turns to Allah in a state of worship and prayers are recited with a pace that match perfectly with my inner rhythm. I know it seems strange, my observation, but I must say that in other masjid I had sometimes to adjust myself to a fast speed in the reciting which creates confusion in me, and makes me wonder what's the purpose of that rush.

In conclusion, thank you to everybody at ICLI for being a living example of Muslim values and practices without being "parochial."

HASSAN HATHOUT, M.D., Ph.D.

Dr. Hassan Hathout is former professor and chairman of Obstetrics and Gynecology at Kuwait and other universities. For the past 12 years he has headed the Outreach Department at Islamic Center of Southern California. He is also a gifted Islamic scholar, speaker, writer, ethicist, poet – among other things. His book, "Reading the Muslim Mind," proved a very potent *dawa* tool.

I believe Islamic Centers have brains, just like people do. Having visited so many centers, I believe that ICLI's is one of the topmost. It acts upon a 21st-century mentality, thanks to enlightened leadership and intelligent community. Of their features I like is their double use of a Sunday for education of both adults and children (separate morning and afternoon programs), their presence in the American life and concerns, and the love they ooze within and without towards Muslims and non-Muslims. Their "sisters' group" is exemplary.

MURAD WILFRIED HOFMANN

Dr. Murad Wilfried Hofmann was born in 1931 into a Catholic family in Aschaffenburg, Germany, where he spent the war years experiencing strategic bombing, siege by General Patton's army, and military occupation. His university education began in 1950 at Union College, Schenectady, N.Y., where he majored in sociology and economics. In 1957, he completed his legal studies of German Law at Munich University with a doctorate in jurisprudence. He pursued his studies of American law at Harvard Law School, leading to a Master's degree in 1960 – and marriage with an American lady. From 1961 – 1994 Dr. Hofmann served in the German Foreign Service specializing on issues of defense and nuclear deterrence. His last assignments were:

- Director of NATO and Defense Affairs in Bon (1979-1983)
- Director of Information for NATO at Brussels (1983-1987)
- Ambassador to Algeria (1987-1990)
- Ambassador to Morocco (1994)

In 1980, he embraced Islam, performing the first one of five *umrahs* in 1982 and *hajj* in 1992. In 1985 he published his "Diary of a German Muslim" (3rd German ed. 1998), also available in English, French and Arabic (Al-Ahram). When his second book, "Islam: The Alternative," appeared in 1992 Dr. Hofmann was viciously attacked as a "fundamentalist" by media and leftist feminists in Germany. The book is available in English, American (amana), Bosnian and several Arabic versions. Amana Publications also published his next books: "Islam 2000" (1996), "Journey to Makkah" (1998), and "Islam in the Third Millenium" (April 2000).

Dr. Hofmann is a regular contributor to "The Muslim World Book Review" and "Encounters" in the U.K., "Islamic Studies" in Pakistan, "Al-Islam" in Germany, and "The American Journal for Islamic Social Studies." He is also a corresponding member of the Royal Academy of Jordan and the 1998 recipient of the annual Islamic Outreach Award from the Islamic Information Service in Los Angeles.

Travelling around the world fi-s-sabil Allah, *I always enjoy Muslim hospitality, courtesy, respect and solidarity, wherever I go. Yet, when visiting the Islamic Center of Long Island in Westbury, New York, I encountered something additional –* happy *people working in a* bright *and* dynamic *atmosphere. Already before entering the mosque I was struck by its integration into a clean, green, well-to-do neighborhood. My overall impression was that Islam, in this building, was practiced at an intellectually high level – among grown-ups and among youngsters. When later on I learned that all this was the result of a long and protracted effort by a handful of Muslim immigrant students, I became envious: What a wonderful feeling it must be to know that one has planted a model island of Islam on an island in America.*

ABDULAH KARCIC

Professor Abdulah Karcic was born in Bosnia and Herzegovina – former Yugoslavia. All his education he received in the capital Sarajevo. At the University of Sarajevo he first graduated at the School of Philosophy and later on at the School of Economics.

Most of his career Professor Karcic spent with Energoinvest, the largest state-owned industrial conglomerate (55,000 employees) in former Yugoslavia. On his foreign postings he traveled worldwide and spent abroad many years with his family. He is fluent in English and German.

Professor Karcic and his family went through the trials and tribulations of the bloody war in Bosnia and Herzegovina. Currently, he lives with his family in New York.

I visited ICLI for the first time in 1995, soon after my arrival to the U.S. What I found there made me a regular visitor.

This Center has many things to offer, covering numerous religious, social and cultural needs of the growing Muslim community. To me, most attractive are presentations held regularly as a part of a Sunday program for adults. Such a variety of topics and speakers are definitely not to be found in other Centers.

In a constructive, polemical atmosphere and dialogue, ICLI is truly an open forum for exchange of diverse viewpoints and thoughts. Many renowned guest speakers include Muslim and non-Muslim scholars, politicians, journalists, novelists, diplomats, and social leaders. Another wonderful notion is that ICLI avoids being a social club of only one ethnic-national group, but welcomes all. That is what gives the Center a tremendous magnetic power, which attracts visitors to come again and again.

MERVE KAVACHI

Ms. Merve Kavachi was elected to the Turkish Parliament. However, she was not permitted to take the oath of office because of her dress code. (She wears a head scarf.) Several years earlier she had to leave medical school for the same reason. Ms. Kavachi, who received some of her education in the USA, is currently engaged in informing Muslims and non-Muslims about the status of human rights in Turkey. She was a guest speaker at the annual dinner of ICLI in October 2000.

I was particularly pleased to see a vibrant, self-confident Islamic community, which is aware of its rights, within the pluralistic, Democratic American society. I believe your biggest asset is this recognition and your approach to taking your true place in American society not with a defeatist psychology based on the distrust to others, but with belief that it will take persistent efforts to reach outward and show the true face of Islam, Muslims to America.

It was also refreshing to see an Islamic community, where women actively participate in all levels of activities not merely to counter the stereotypes of women's role in Islamic societies but from the recognition of their talents and capacities to contribute to Dawah and welfare of Muslim community.

From my conversations during our ICLI visit as well as those with other Islamic communities, I realize that Islamic community in America is not a monolithic bloc owing to many reasons including differences in ethnicity, culture, education levels, affluence and in interpretations of Islam, and its practice in America. Your community is obviously one of the more liberal and more sophisticated communities that approach to issues from a pragmatic perspective. There are others which may be more "fundamentalist." I think it is incumbent upon the leaders of all communities to try to be inclusive and not dismiss the validity of different approaches so that our efforts may be concentrated on the most fundamental issues on which all Muslims agree upon.

<u>ROBERT F. KEELER</u>

Mr. Robert F. Keeler is the religion writer for *Newsday* and a *Pulitzer Prize* awardee.

Every time I set foot in the Islamic Center of Long Island, the thing that strikes me most forcefully is the lovely rainbow of people that greets me – people from so many cultures, of so many shades of skin, with so many different backgrounds, accents, life stories, styles of cuisine and fashion. As different as they all are in so many ways, everyone at this masjid is exactly alike in one important dimension: They all display an unfailing warmth of hospitality, toward Muslim and non-Muslim alike.

Their Sunday morning educational programs attract an intensely interested group, full of curiosity and energy, but also elaborately courteous in questioning guest speakers. I have always come away from these events feeling appreciated for whatever information I was able to convey, but also feeling stimulated to think more clearly on the issues we had discussed.

If I were Muslim, this is the place where I would choose to worship.

STEPHEN AND SHELLEY LIMMER

Mr. Stephen Limmer is a former President of the Temple Beth El, while Ms. Shelly Limmer is the current President of the Temple. Both are active supporters and contributors of AMJID.

It is hard to capture the change in our lives and thoughts as a result of our friendship and what we have learned through our participation in AMJID. The Islamic Center of Long Island has been an integral part of building essential Muslim and Jewish dialogue through AMJID, American Muslims and Jews in Dialogue. For more than eight years, at the mosque, Temple Beth-El in Great Neck, and members' homes, we have shared our common beliefs, concerns, and goals, while we tried to understand and respect our different creeds, scriptures, and understandings of history. Both our groups representing peoples who have suffered in this country from prejudice, yet shared in all of the freedoms that America has to offer as a true land of liberty, whose practices do not always live up to its ideals. Our commonalties range from our desire for peace in the Middle East, to dealing with our children's reaction to Christmas all around them, to raising the necessary money for the annual operating budgets for our respective mosque and synagogue. We each seek peace, and understanding, and the freedom to allow all people to find their own way to the One who created us all. We thank the Islamic Center and its leaders, like Faroque and Arfa Khan, who have helped break down walls of ignorance, prejudice, stereotyping, and fear, and enabled us to see all of the dreams for humanity which we share, and to provide us with new, respected, and lasting friends.

ANISA MEHDI

Ms. Anisa Mehdi is President of Whetstone Productions, which specializes in television production and reporting. Ms. Mehdi is a contributing correspondent to the PBS news program *Religion and Ethics News Weekly*. In March 1998 she made an unprecedented journey to Makkah to report on the Hajj for *Religion and Ethics News Weekly*, becoming the first American producer/reporter to do so.

My experience with the Center is limited, yet profound.

Firstly, I am most grateful to Brother Ghazi Khankan and the ICLI for the February 1999 tribute to my late father, El Marhoum Dr. Mohammad T. Mehdi, which memorialized the anniversary of his passing.

Secondly, I am impressed with the political activism and participation generated by ICLI. As a reporter/producer for PBS's "Religion and Ethics News Weekly" I covered the October 1998 conference of the American Muslim Alliance in Hempstead, NY. I know that the success of that event is owed in part to the efforts of the ICLI. I am also aware of the weekly letters and e-mails coming from the Center, urging people to write to their representatives in Washington, DC and to respond appropriately to media reports on Islam and the Muslim community.

Lastly, I am appreciative of the materials I receive from ICLI, including Islamic calendars to complement my Julian diary, notices about special events, and schedules for fasting during Ramadan. ICLI is providing an important service in this way.

DR. NAWAL NOUR

Sudanese-American, Harvard-trained Ob/Gyn specialist who has developed a national and international reputation for her work in the field of female circumcision (FC) and female genital mutilation (FGM) in Boston, Massachusetts.

It was very interesting to know what the ICLI does and how large its members are. I am also impressed that you were willing to have me as your speaker. The topic of FC/FGM is a difficult one and I think it shows how open-minded your organization is to have it discussed that evening. I was even more honored to be selected amongst two other distinguished women who are doing phenomenal work in their fields. It was a pleasure to meet you and your board.

MARGHOOB QURAISHI

Marghoob Quraishi is a very active member of the Muslim community. A certified management consultant with vast experience in management, Mr. Quraishi has several firsts to his long list of achievements. He was founder of the Muslim Youth Camp, Stanford Islamic School, Muslim Student Association and, most recently, Muslim Student Network (MSN). His initiation of MSN brought him into contact with ICLI, which has been supporting the MSN.

There are approximately 1,600 Islamic centers in the United States. Islamic Center of Long Island (ICLI) is somewhat unique. Because of its various expanding programs, ICLI stands out as a shining example for other centers to follow.

In addition to serving religious, educational, cultural and social needs of the community, which other centers also do, the forward-looking leadership of ICLI is looking beyond the confines of local Muslim community, as well as what lies beyond the horizon. It is building closer ties with other non-Muslim communities in the country which are fighting against human rights abuses worldwide. In addition, it is actively supporting other national groups that are engaged in such activities which eventually would help contribute Islamic values in American political discourse.

One good example of such support is *Muslim Student Network (MSN)* which ICLI has been supporting for the last two years. *MSN, a two-month-long annual summer internship program held in Washington, D.C., is a leadership training program designed to train a new team of leaders who will build an expanding network of a dynamic cadre of young Muslim "movers and shakers" serving Islam and Muslims in America.*

IRVING AND BOBBIE ROSENZWEIG

Irving and Bobbie Rosenzweig are two active participants of the highly successful *American Muslims and Jews in Dialogue* program.

We are members of the American Muslims and Jews in Dialogue (AMJID) – a group of representatives from the ICLI and from our Temple Beth-El of Great Neck, a Jewish synagogue. AMJID was started about eight years ago to encourage and develop an understanding and acceptance of two groups of Americans who knew very little about each other. The ICLI welcomed the opportunity to become involved with people of a different faith.

Over the years, we have reached out to each other in many different ways. We have learned about the other's religion, culture, history, heritage and problems. We've recognized and accepted our differences. We've been amazed at our similarities. We have become friends.

It has been, and hopefully will continue to be, a rewarding and enlightening experience for both of our religious institutions and their people. For Muslim and for Jew – the horizons have expanded.

HABIBULLAH SALEEM

Habibullah Saleem, a Muslim by way of the leadership of Imam Warith Deen Mohammad. Educator, writer, consultant, and author of seven books, including those for inspiring and educating our youth. Graduate of Benedict College, Columbia, South Carolina. While now conducting his own cable T.V. show called Reaching, Teaching and Learning, received the key to the city of Pontiac, Michigan, for inspiring the students at Pontiac High School. Mr. Saleem is presently the Director of Communications in schools at Cleveland Elementary in Newark, New Jersey. Taught the children of Muhammad Ali, our former World Boxing Champion. Mr. Saleem has also held the position of school principal in numerous Muslim schools. For lectures and workshops, he can be reached at (973) 282-1480; e-mail ClevelandHF@MindSpring.com.

(With the name *Allah*)
HOW TO MANAGE A SUCCESSFUL MOSQUE
By: Habibullah Saleem

People management is like a master key
Unlocking minds for people to be free
Techniques and strategies so valuable they are
Managing the mosque while promoting "Allah"
Inviting new people to learn and grow
The truth of Al Islam we want them to know
The Imam of the mosque insightful and keen
Relating to the people the essence of the deen
Courtesy and kindness a welcoming skill
Managing to increase the people's will
Recognizing levels and differences of thought
Management is successful when the people are taught
Muslims believing – Muslims with faith
Producing and producing, setting the pace
Explaining in detail the basics with facts
Planning intelligently to become exact
Calling the adhan, calling on time
Rushing to salat to avoid decline
Establishing an environment, an environment of trust
Involved in the community with understanding and thrust
Thinking big with small things in check
Striving in righteousness to be correct
Eliminating gossip or slanderous talk
Illegal procedure is known as a balk
Confidential conversation remaining concealed
To all people of the world "Allah" appeals
Male or female, a religion for both
Accepting Shahadah by taking an oath
Learning from the Quran about self and others
All categories of life, the Quran, it covers
Defining marriage and the dangers of divorce
Appropriate management means being on course
And so in the mosque flexible and firm
Appropriate management so the people can learn
Clinging to failure while progress dies
Teaching the truth while living lies
Strong in criticism but weak in execution
Like making Salat without ablution
Management in the masjid, Imam or other

139

In proper management "Allah" will uncover
Controlling minds is not the answer
The body of the mosque will end up with cancer
And so the key is to obey "Allah"
Management in the mosque means management up to par
Allahu Akbar!

FREDERICK A. SMITH, M.D.

Dr. Frederick A. Smith is Senior Associate Chief of the Division of General Internal Medicine at New York University School of Medicine. Dr. Smith is an Assistant Professor of Clinical Medicine.

I have made several Friday afternoon visits to ICLI, each time as mentor to a group of young doctors whom I teach in the internal medicine residency training program at North Shore University Hospital in Manhasset. The visits have been hosted by Dr. Faroque Khan as part of a course titled "Religion and Medicine," in which, over a period of six weeks, the residents are exposed to salient religious ideas, cultural variations and perspectives on health and illness of the worlds' great religious traditions.

The goal of the program is to increase these doctors' knowledge, sensitivity and respect for the religious views of patients of different backgrounds, and to help them understand how their patients' views may impact on medical treatment both during illness and at the end of life. The medical residents, themselves, some of whom are children of immigrants, come from a variety of religious backgrounds including Christian, Jewish, Muslim, Hindu and Buddhist traditions. For almost all who are not Muslim, this constituted the first visit to a mosque.

Our visits to ICLI have begun with the Friday sermon and prayer service. For a devoutly religious person like me who comes from an Abrahamic tradition, the preacher's theme of authentically following God's will strikes a responsive chord. The congregation's united prayer, within the mosque's architecturally spare but beautiful setting, clearly resonates as the direct, unmediated worship of the same God to whom I pray and whom I desire to obey: the God of Abraham, of Sarah, Isaac and Moses; of Haggar and Ishmael; of Jesus the Christ; of the prophet Mohammed.

The hospitality we experienced was heartfelt and complete, down to the lunch and dessert offered during our didactic session with Dr. Khan after the service. Dr. Khan explained the origins, the basic tenets and the cultural diversity of Islam, and the religion's perspective on issues of health and illness, death and burial, autopsy and organ donation. He then answered any and all questions (including why women sit in the back, and how to counsel diabetic patients about diet and medication during Ramadan).

I believe we have all left the mosque with a new understanding and deep respect for the religion of Islam, a better understanding of how to approach the health issues of our Muslim patients, and a melting of any remaining negative stereotypes about Muslims (which are unfortunately too easy to imbibe in American culture today). We appreciate – if we did not already – that Islamic society and religion are not monolithic, that the entire religion should no more be tarred by the negative acts of a few of its members than should any other religion, and that the worshippers who welcomed us into their worship are fellow human beings and fellow Americans who share with us the desire to attain and preserve "the full blessings of liberty. . . endowed to us by our Creator" which our country stands for at its best.

SAYYID M. SYEED, Ph.D.

Dr. Sayyid M. Syeed is the Secretary General of the Islamic Society of North America, the largest Muslim umbrella organization in North America. The annual ISNA convention has an attendance of over thirty thousand Muslims.

I was very pleased to know that you have decided to chronicle the growth and development of the ICLI. Congratulations to you for this resolve and Insha Allah, it is going to be a rewarding experience. We have people who are engrossed in making history and others who are busy in writing history, but there are few who are doing both. I am glad that you are going to be among those few, Insha Allah.

My visit to your center has reinforced my faith in a historical role of Muslim communities in America. They are a source of blessings for themselves and a source of blessings for the American mainstream. Your center is strategically located and Allah has blessed you with the right kind of human resources. Your experiences, successes and failures will be tremendously valuable for other similar groups engaged in a similar task of building institutions in America.

MICHAEL WOLFE

Michael Wolfe is the author of numerous books of poetry, fiction, and travel writing. Over the past 12 years he has produced two books about Islam. *The Hajj: An American's Pilgrimage to Mecca,* is Wolfe's first-hand account of a five-month journey to Mecca. His latest work, *Journey with a Thousand Roads*, (Grove/Atlantic, Fall 1997) is a collection of Hajj accounts by two dozen travelers to Mecca, spanning the last thousand years. In April 1997, *ABC News* selected Wolfe to write and help produce a half-hour program for Ted Koppel's *Nightline* show. The program was shot in Saudi Arabia where Wolfe traveled with a small film crew, presenting the Hajj and its week-long set of rites as he performed them. The program, <u>the first of its kind in the United States,</u> was broadcast nationally, with Ted Koppel (in Washington, DC) and Michael Wolfe (in Mecca) narrating.

The following statement made by *Atlantic Monthly Press*, the publisher of *The Hajj*, alludes to the exquisite work accomplished by Mr. Wolfe. "Not since Sir Richard Burton's account of the pilgrimage to Mecca over a century ago has a Western writer described *the Hajj* in such stunning and intimate detail. At a time when the eyes of the world are on Islam, *The Hajj* offers a perceptive and much-needed look at its human face."

Faroque Khan's book is long overdue. It catalogues and helps interpret from a Muslim point of view the long, crucial development of one of the most productive Islamic Centers in the United States. Someday, Americans will look back upon this history and see it as the miracle it is. Today, Dr. Khan's book is worth more than gold for its clear presentation of the process by which Muslims of all backgrounds are adding a community of enormous value to the Greater New York area. Its non-Muslim neighbors have benefited greatly too. The section on American Muslims and Jews in Dialogue is especially valuable. Anyone TRULY interested in community building should read this book.

Chapter 13

ELECTION 2000: THE ROLE OF AMERICAN MUSLIMS

The November 2000 presidential election in the USA will be remembered for many unique features; and for the Muslim community, it represented a moment of maturity, coordination, and the flexing of its growing political influence. This election resulted in:

- Republican candidate George W. Bush winning the electoral-college vote, while the Democratic candidate Albert Gore won the popular vote. Americans, many for the first time, understood the difference between the Electoral College and the popular vote.
- In the United States Senate, an equal number of Republicans and Democrats won seats, resulting in a 50-50 split in the Senate. The tie-breaking vote will be provided by the Vice President – Republican Richard Cheney.
- In the United States House of Representatives, the Republicans have a slight edge with 51% of the seats.

Thus, the two branches of government - the Executive and the Legislative - will have Republicans in the lead. Traditionally, the Republicans lean towards the "right," while the Democrats lean towards the "left" of center. How the left-of-center, popular-vote majority will play out with the right-of-center elected Executive and Legislative branches will be very interesting to observe.

To the credit of the Senate leadership, for the first time there will be power-sharing arrangements with equal representation by the Republicans and Democrats on all committees and, even more important, equal distribution of resources for staff and space. Thus, there is hope that the elected leadership will work together in advancing the important issues in the USA and abroad.

The prolonged legislative and legal "battle" in the State of Florida, after the votes were cast on November 7th, taught us terms such as hanging chads, pregnant chads, and butterfly ballots, and created an

143

unparalleled and unprecedented interest in our nation's political process. Hopefully, this experience in Florida will result in a major overhaul of the ballot-counting system, leading to a uniform, reproducible, easily accessible system.

For American Muslims there were several firsts, as well:

- For the first time an essentially Muslim issue was brought up in a presidential debate when Governor Bush brought it up in the second debate on October 11, 2000 in Missouri. Bush pointed out that Muslims, particularly Arab-Americans, are the new victims of racial profiling. He was referring to the secret-evidence act under which many Muslims have been imprisoned without their having access to the charges brought against them.

- This was the first time Muslims turned out to vote in big numbers, with an estimated 34-40% voting for the first time. This was the first time that Muslim-American organizations endorsed a candidate as a bloc vote.

- Over 700 Muslims ran for various offices, of whom 152 got elected.

- The Republicans worked on winning the Muslim votes. They hired a Muslim political activist to liaison better with the community, and the leadership of the Republican Party met with the coordinating council of Muslim organizations.

That is not to say that all Muslims voted across the board for Republicans. While over 70% of the voters voted for President Bush and Vice President Cheney, there was widespread ticket splitting in other cases. A dramatic example of this occurred in the New York State Senate race where overwhelming numbers (more than 95%) of Muslims voted for the Democratic candidate Hillary R. Clinton.

In the enclosed articles, some key aspects of this campaign are highlighted:

1. Congressman Paul Findley's special report in the January/February 2001 issue of *The Washington Report on Middle East Affairs* titled "American Muslims Demonstrate Unity, Influence with Historic Bloc Vote." This analysis clearly states that without the 64,000 additional Muslim votes in the State of Florida, Mr. Bush would not have won that state and the Presidency.

2. The New York Senate race presented some very unique challenges for the community. Two articles - *The Battle of Jericho* by Eric Vickers, and *Muslims in New York: A Moment of Awakening and Reckoning* published in "The Muslim Observer," December 22-28, 2000, and authored by me - summarize the strategy, methodology, and the results of the active Muslim participation in the Election 2000.

Clearly Muslim-Americans have set an example for a higher level of participation, and now there is no choice but to move ahead and participate more vigorously in national public life. The role of centers such as ICLI will be to develop and guide Muslims and educate them in the system of government, and have the membership engage in an active dialogue with all representatives at the local village, county, state, and national level.

We are hopeful, based on our experience on Long Island and in New York, that Muslims are prepared for and eager to take up the challenge and help make a difference for the better in the USA.

In a sample of voters in New York, we found 74% voted for Bush/Cheney, 18% for Ralph Nader, and 8% for Al Gore, while over 95% voted for Democratic Senatorial candidate Hillary R. Clinton.

American Muslims Demonstrate Unity, Influence With Historic Bloc Vote
By Paul Findley

George W. Bush should thank Florida Muslims for opening his way to the White House. Responding to a national campaign, they discarded normal Democratic Party allegiance and voted as a bloc for the Republican from Texas, providing him with a statewide net gain in Florida of more than 64,000 Muslim votes.

Had they not voted as a bloc, Vice President Al Gore would have emerged as the clear winner shortly after the polls closed on Nov. 7. There would have been no recounts, no long, divisive wrangling in state and federal courts. Even with dimpled ballots left uncounted, Gore's Florida total would have substantially topped the Texas governor's, giving the vice president the majority of the nation's electoral votes and quick certification as president-elect.

A June poll showed a slight national Muslim preference for Gore, but an intensive campaign that began on Sept. 3 transformed Muslim sympathies into a nine-to-one landslide for Bush when votes were counted. In Florida, the state that proved pivotal in the ultimate certification of the president-elect, Bush's Muslim margin was even greater.

The importance of Muslim bloc voting arises from its magnitude, as well as its focus. Best estimates put the national Muslim population at seven million, 70 as the percentage of those eligible to vote, and 65 as the percentage of those eligible who actually voted. This means that the national turnout of Muslims on Nov. 7 came to 3.2 million.

According to an exit poll of 1,774 Muslims, 72 percent voted for Bush and 8 percent for Gore. This means an estimated 2.3 million Muslims voted for Bush and only 256,000 for Gore, a national net gain for Bush in excess of two million.

The Muslim impact in Florida was even more impressive. Accepting the assumptions used in the national analysis and 200,000 as the Muslim population in Florida, 140,000 Muslims were eligible and 91,000 actually voted. If 80 percent – a conservative estimate – supported Bush, this means he received 72,000 Muslim votes. If 8 percent – a generous estimate – voted for Gore, his total vote came to 7,238. In Florida, the net Muslim vote for Bush topped 64,000. Of the total Muslim vote, 26,000 were from first-time voters. The national exit poll of Muslims showed that 36 percent cast ballots for the first time.

A December 1999 survey of Muslim voters showed only 25 percent for Bush.

Muslims entered the presidential arena in earnest because they were troubled by challenges to their civil rights at home and to their inter-

146

ests in the Holy Land - especially Jerusalem. They responded to these issues rather than to party or personality. Early in the year, polls showed the Democratic Party more popular among Muslims than the Republican Party. Their hearts, however, belonged to Green Party candidate Ralph Nader, who condemned Israel for excessive force against Palestinian protesters and was the first Arab American to run for president.

Although sympathetic to a number of Gore's domestic positions, Muslims were upset over his attachment to Israel, particularly his unequivocal acceptance of Jerusalem as its exclusive capital, and what they perceived as his lack of concern for the plight of Palestinians. Muslims see Israel's control of East Jerusalem as a continuing threat to Haram al-Sharif, one of Islam's holiest shrines.

On election day, Muslims pinned their hopes for improved Middle East policies on Bush and were pleased when he promised to halt the use of secret evidence in deportation hearings, a policy Muslims considered especially offensive because they viewed it as directed mainly at their community.

The most important factor that led Muslims to vote as a bloc for Bush was the unity and perseverance of the leaders of four principal public policy organizations: the American Muslim Alliance (AMA), the Council of American-Islamic Relations (CAIR), the American Muslim Council (AMC), and the Muslim Public Affairs Council (MPAC). In participating, two of the leaders – Dr. Agha Saeed, founder and chairman of AMA and the chief engineer of Muslim bloc voting, and Salam Al-Marayati, national director of MPAC – departed from their customary allegiance to the Democratic Party. CAIR was represented by Omar Ahmad and Nihad Awad and AMC by Yahya Basha, M.D.

Banding together at the American Muslim Political Coordination Council (AMPCC), they organized voter-education and registration drives early in the spring primary campaigns. In the late spring and summer of 2000, they sponsored workshops in major cities for candidates, campaign volunteers, and prospective voters.

Over Labor Day weekend at Chicago's O'Hare Airport, they won enthusiastic support for bloc voting for president from an audience of more than 10,000 Muslims. Hoping for personal interviews with both Bush and Gore, they delayed their recommendation for president until two weeks before Election Day.

One Met, The Other Didn't

Their decision followed an interview with Bush in Detroit on Oct. 5, during which he promised to listen to their policy concerns. Gore canceled a scheduled interview. News of their endorsement was circulated

147

through e-mails, notices in mosques and Islamic centers, and sermons by imams during congregational prayers on the Friday before the election.

In supporting Bush, many Muslims followed the example of Saeed and Al-Marayati by departing from traditional party leanings. In June, a CAIR survey of Muslims in 37 states showed that 31 percent believed the Democratic Party best represented their interests. Only 17 percent favored the Republican Party. Forty-three percent said they were either undecided or believed that neither major party was addressing their basic Muslim interests.

Bush started from a low point in his 11-month climb to a Muslim landslide. A series of national surveys conducted by CAIR's director of research, Dr. Mohamed Nimer, marked his progress. In December 1999, the eve of the 2000 primary elections, a survey of 734 eligible Muslim voters showed only 25 percent for Bush. Fifteen percent favored Democrat Bill Bradley and 15 percent were in Gore's corner. When Bradley dropped out as a candidate four months later, most of his Muslim support went to Gore. In June, a poll of 755 Muslims showed 33 percent for Gore, with Bush up slightly at 28 percent.

In the final eight weeks of the campaign, Muslim support for Bush nearly doubled. A September survey of 1,022 eligible voters showed a 12 percent increase for the Texas governor: 40 percent for Bush, 25 percent Nader, and 24 percent Gore. On Election Day, most of the Nader and Gore votes moved to Bush.

Bloc voting marks the arrival of Muslims as a new, national political power, but it was little noted until the votes were counted. During the presidential campaign, Muslims were largely ignored by Gore, and, despite their near-unanimous turnout for Bush, they received relatively little attention during the Texas governor's quest for votes.

He made only one public statement that bestirred Muslims - his criticism of secret evidence - but it may have been enough to win him many votes, especially in Florida. The controversy had long been a raging, much-publicized issue among Muslims nationally, but nowhere else with as much intensity as in Florida. The reason for this focus was the plight of Dr. Mazen Al-Najjar, a Muslim Palestinian on the faculty of the University of South Florida, who had been locked up in a Bradenton jail for three and one-half years. In proceedings before a U.S. immigration court, evidence that he was not allowed to see was sufficient to convince the judge that he was guilty of supporting terrorist organizations in the Middle East. Al-Najjar denied the allegation, and his attorneys protested vainly that the secret policy effectively denied him due process. He was charged with holding a lapsed student visa and held without bond while he fought against deportation. He finally was released on bond in mid-December.

As political leaders study the 2000 election returns, they should gain a more accurate appreciation of America's Muslim community and, accordingly, make changes in their tactics in future campaigning for most offices, not just the presidency. During the year, 700 Muslims were candidates for offices ranging from convention delegate and precinct committeemen to membership in state legislatures. The list includes both Republicans and Democrats. One hundred and fifty-two, including a state senate candidate and two candidates for state representative, were victorious.

After analyzing Muslim voting, Agha Saeed declared, "In this year's election, U.S. Muslims crossed the political Rubicon."

Paul Findley served from 1981-1983 as a U.S. Representative from Illinois. He is the author of the best seller, "They Dare to Speak Out: People and Institutions Confront Israel's Lobby." His book, "Silent No More: Confronting America's False Images of Islam," is scheduled for publication in 2001 by Amana Publications. Congressman Findley resides in Jacksonville, Illilnois.

THE BATTLE OF JERICHO: MUSLIMS TAKE A STAND

In the annals of American political history, the national elections of the year 2000 will be recorded as having many facets, but none more overriding than it being a referendum on the presidency of Bill Clinton. Historians will see this reflected both in the presidential contest and in the contest waged in New York by his wife, Hillary, for a seat in the U.S. Senate.

In the annals of world history, the elections of the year 2000 will be recorded as the year Muslims became a permanent and significant factor in American politics. As with many historical events, this watershed event began with a single step that quickly evolved into a phenomenon through forces and consequences unforeseen.

History will record that in October 2000 Muslims in America united in an unprecedented fashion to endorse a candidate for the presidency. A newly formed umbrella organization, the American Muslim Political Coordinating Council (AMPCC), consisting of most of the major Muslim organizations involved in national and local politics agreed, as a demonstration of unity, to support the candidacy of the Republican presidential candidate, George W. Bush, and as a strategy to work on his behalf in the key electoral states that could swing the election. No sooner had this historic event been made public at a press conference in the nation's capital than an assault against Muslim political involvement commenced in the country's most prestigious city and in the state where the eyes of the nation were focused on the Senate race. New York soon and unexpectedly became the battleground of the Muslims' struggle for political participation.

The campaign to deny Muslims political enfranchisement and legitimacy was traceable to an event held earlier that summer in Boston - the birthplace of the American Revolution. The event was by all measure a normal political fundraiser being held for the benefit of Hillary's Senate campaign. What made the event unique, however, was that it was being sponsored by an organization founded for the purpose of politically empowering Muslim Americans, the American Muslim Alliance (AMA), and that a significant amount of funds were raised ($50,000). In accordance with federal election laws, this amount was raised entirely through individual contributions, which was publicly reported shortly after the event.

Several months later, in late October, as the elections were entering their final stage and heating up, Hillary's opponent, Rick Lazio, after apparently being fed information by known anti-Muslim operatives, seized upon this as an issue to court the powerful Jewish vote in New York. He went public with dogmatic denunciations of Hillary for taking money he described as "blood money" from "Muslim organizations" he alleged espoused terrorism. The New York media leapt at the story, commencing an investigation of funds received by Hillary not only from the AMA Boston event, but funds received as well from a prominent figure of another longstanding American Muslim organization, the American Muslim Council (AMC).

In the midst of this political swirl of events were world events, captured daily by the media, which seemed to be spinning out of control. The peace process in the Middle East had collapsed and virtual warfare was at hand over the issue of Palestine and Jerusalem. Seventeen U.S. sailors had been killed on the U.S.S. Cole in what was widely portrayed by the media as a terrorist attack by certain Muslim groups in the Middle East. Thus, Lazio's charges of Hillary's Muslim connection were akin to pouring kerosene on a blazing fire.

Fearing the possible loss of needed Jewish support, Hillary quickly disavowed her ties with Muslims by returning the $50,000 in contributions and publicly disclaiming any attachment to the AMA and AMC.

Initially, the Muslim community was stunned, even hurt by Hillary's abrupt disavowal, because she had up to that time expressed empathy for Muslim issues. The community seemed resigned to once again endure the pain of being rejected and stereotyped by mainstream powers, opting to only fight back through press statements and op-ed letters denying the scurrilous accusations.

But in a manner completely unplanned, the situation rapidly escalated exponentially to a point where the Muslim community was compelled into an all-out confrontation. Under the auspices of the Republican Party, Lazio supporters engaged in a telephone-bank operation in which over a half million New Yorkers were called and told, in essence, that the American Muslims who had donated to Hillary were responsible for the terrorist attack on the U.S.S. Cole. Hillary was infuriated; the Muslims outraged.

Now the Muslims realized that only an all-out campaign to defeat and discredit Lazio could vindicate them and permit their unconditional acceptance by the American political system. The AMA dispatched a Board member to New York to manage in the final week of the election the "Defeat Lazio" campaign. Working with the President of the New York Long Island AMA Chapter, Dr. Faroque Khan, they organized from his home in Jericho, New York a full-fledged campaign to mobilize the Muslims in New York to vote against Lazio.

151

Meetings with Imams, other Muslim leaders, and Muslim organizations like the Muslim taxi drivers, were hastily carried out during the week. Alliances were formed with interfaith organizations, which also publicly denounced Lazio's bigotry. A sense of urgency and unity of purpose was impressed upon the community – a unity that crossed all the usual lines of ethnic origin and race division. Information about the campaign was disseminated through telephone trees, E-mailings, literature distribution, meetings at mosques and elsewhere, word of mouth, and press conferences.

Early polls indicated that Lazio's Muslim bashing tactic was working. Polls that had before shown Hillary leading were now registering that her votes were slipping, and other polls showed Lazio taking a slight lead. But the tide began to shift when the Muslims began to counter Lazio publicly, and when Lazio was put on the defensive by Dr. Khan revealing to the media several Lazio fundraising letters he had received, casting Lazio, in the eyes of the media, as a hypocrite. The Muslim community became energized in an unprecedented fashion. Energized to the point where a protest demonstration was held in front of the campaign office of Lazio, a demonstration in which over 100 participated, including Muslim children who held up posters stating, "Muslims are here to stay."

While the "Defeat Lazio" campaign was in high gear, the Muslim community demonstrated political savvy by maintaining a bridge with Hillary through Muslims active in the Democratic Party, who conveyed to her and her staff the community's great disappointment, but also a willingness to dialogue following the election.

Major stories about this issue ran daily in all the New York newspapers and was featured as the lead story in most of the vast TV coverage. All this extensive effort and publicity culminated in the November 5, 2000 Newsday newspaper headline "Muslim Issue Dominates Senate Race."

While the outcome of the Senate race was clearly of importance to the Muslim community, history will record that what was of even more importance was the manner in which Muslims rallied to the cause. History will also record that under such circumstances, nothing less could be expected of people of such a faith.

Eric Erfan Vickers
Board Member, American Muslim Alliance

MUSLIMS IN NEW YORK: A MOMENT OF AWAKENING AND RECKONING

Published in *Muslim Observer*, Vol. 11, Issue 51, Page 6
By Faroque Khan

The New York Senate race between Hillary R. Clinton and Rick Lazio put New York Muslims in a position they never thought would transpire – Muslims became an issue. A brief chronology will help put this in perspective.

On Monday, October 23rd, the American Political Coordinating Council, an umbrella organization which includes four major American Muslim organizations – American Muslim Alliance (AMA), American Muslim Islamic Relations, Muslim Public Affairs Council – endorsed George W. Bush for President. This was the first time that a coordinated Muslim endorsement was given to a presidential candidate. Some folks obviously didn't like this.

Two days later The New York Daily News reported on the $50,000 fundraising event held by AMA in Massachusetts in June 2000 - four months earlier. Mrs. Clinton reportedly returned this money, and Mr. Lazio referred to this as "blood money." This resulted in unprecedented anger among Muslims who had been yearning to join and participate in the political process. Worse was to follow. For several days the main news regarding the New York Senate race focused on Muslims - they became the issue.

As President of the New York State Chapter of AMA, I was contacted by numerous news/TV, etc. people seeking my views regarding this issue - Does AMA support terrorism? Is it a front for overseas organizations? Does it support violence as a means of fighting occupation? Mr. Lazio, in his public pronouncements, continued to associate Muslims with terrorism, and over 500,000 calls were placed on behalf of Mr. Lazio by the New York Republican Party informing New Yorkers that somehow Muslims were involved in the USS Cole attack. This was the final straw. "We don't want your money," "Your mainstream organizations are terrorist fronts," and "You are somehow connected with the attack on the USS Cole."

While Mr. Lazio continued to vilify and attack Muslims, I received over a dozen letters from Mr. Lazio soliciting campaign contributions. This hypocritical behavior of Mr. Lazio was headlined on all major New York papers and television shows, and became the lead story on November 1st and *The New York Times'* article on November 2nd read, "Lazio is Put on Defensive Over the Muslim Issue." The smear campaign of Mr. Lazio had other consequences that I never predicted or imagined.

Numerous calls from non-Muslims who expressed support for us at this time of crisis were greatly appreciated. Many said they had changed their vote because of this hypocrisy. The Muslim community's anger and energy were channeled into one issue - Defeat Lazio. The following is a synopsis of how the community responded.

Let Lazio Know:

I placed an Internet message to the 40-plus New York Muslims on my mailing list with a request for them to send the message to others and call Mr. Lazio's office (provided the phone number) with the following message:

> "You have lost my vote because you are engaged in a hate campaign against American Muslims. You should apologize to American Muslims for engaging in low-down, dirty, hate politics."

Thousands of calls poured into Mr. Lazio's office. It was clear his staff was very irritated with these persistent calls. On Sunday, November 3rd, led by the Bay Shore Muslim community (where Lazio's congressional office is located), several hundred Muslim children, women and men demonstrated for several hours, denouncing the hypocritical, bigoted campaign of Mr. Lazio. This was carried by the television and print media.

Inform the Muslims:

An advisory was prepared and distributed via the Internet and hand distributed listing the candidates worthy of Muslim support. This resulted in ticket splitting with Bush/Cheney for President/Vice President, and Hillary Clinton for Senate, along with local Assembly/Senate/Town candidates. Just to give an idea of the energy and enthusiasm of this effort, three young Muslims from Queens personally sent 14,000 e-mails and distributed 10,000 advisory flyers at various masjids, community gatherings, etc.

The Muslim Taxi Drivers' Association was actively involved. Over 10,000 bumper stickers stating, "Muslims for Hillary Clinton," were placed on New York City taxicabs and distributed at gatherings. This massive street blitz was noticed by the Republican Mayor Giuliani's office, which asked one of the key organizers, "What's going on here?" "Don't the Muslims usually vote Republican?"

Mobilize the Vote:

During the week prior to the election at all the public and private gatherings I attended, the sole topic of discussion was strategizing on how to get the maximum number of people to the voting centers. Several hundred taxicabs were available for this, and a large number of volunteers helped accomplish this. It was no surprise to us in New York that a post-election survey of Muslims indicated that almost 40% had voted for the first time.

Publicize the Muslim Perspective:
I was interviewed on National Public Radio, CBS Radio, ABC/Fox Television and major news coverage was provided by *The New York Times*, *The New York Observer*, *Newsday* and others. My message was simple: Muslims are here to stay. It's hypocritical of Mr. Lazio to connect us with terrorists while he continues to ask for our financial support. (I had over a dozen letters of solicitation available for the media.) The New York Times published a special piece, profiling me, on November 3rd under Public Lives and titled "Lexus Republican But No Friend of Lazio." This resulted after a two-hour interview with *The New York Times* reporter.

The bigotry of Mr. Lazio, his entire focus in the final days on overseas issues, and his attempt to broad-brush Muslims as terrorists turned off many voters, plus the entire Muslim community, resulting in an unprecedented landslide defeat with an over-700,000 voter margin. One of Mr. Lazio's senior campaign advisors, commenting on this result, stated: "Mr. Lazio lost the election when he decided to run for the Israeli Knesset instead of the New York State Senate." In late October, polls showed both candidates in a statistical dead heat.

Mr. Lazio has changed the political landscape of New York, and by extension the USA, forever, and we believe for the better. Politicians who continue to ignore, diminish, and insult Muslims will do so at their own peril. Thank you, Mr. Lazio, for awakening a sleeping giant.

Public Profile: A Lexus Republican, but No Friend of Lazio
The New York Times, November 3, 2000
By Robin Finn

MUTTONTOWN, N.Y. - *You're practically neighbors, and there was a time when you might have earned his vote. He's a registered Republican, just like you. But beware, Representative Rick A. Lazio, you've gotten under the skin of the wrong guy. And not just because your Senate campaign keeps sending him that junk mail, or because he had a great time with President Clinton at that White House prayer breakfast in September (no, he didn't sleep in the Lincoln Bedroom). It's those things you've been saying about certain Muslim groups.*

 "My straw poll, and I admit it's biased, tells me Mr. Lazio is going to lose," predicts Dr. Faroque A. Khan, brown eyes tired but mis-

chievous, from his perch on a damask sofa in a formal living room where the special touches – the intricately patterned rug, the hand-painted papier-mâché urns – come from his birthplace, Kashmir.

Dr. Khan, should everybody remove their shoes the way you have? No, no, he says, waving an arm. The carpet may be vintage, but it isn't sacred to him. The right to vote? That is.

The power of the polling place has long held a fascination for Dr. Khan, a physician, Long Island mosque official and grass-roots Muslim political leader who has suddenly found himself in the spotlight because of the blows that two famous Senate candidates have been trading.

Back in Kashmir, elections were a farce. When he left to complete his medical residency at Queens Hospital Center in 1967, Dr. Khan, now 57, brought a memory of what happened when his father, a Harvard-educated engineer, went to cast his vote one year.

"The man who was working at the polls said, `Why have you bothered to come here? You're a government servant. We've already cast your ballot.' " That was why, 30 years ago, Dr. Khan's father ordered him not to come back to Kashmir, but to stay in the United States and make his difference here.

Fast-forward to Long Island, election year 2000, an election that is, according to Dr. Khan, a second defining moment for Muslim Americans.

"The first was the tragedy of the Oklahoma bombing; up until that time, the Muslim community wasn't too bothered with social policy, and then, within 24 hours of allegations of a Muslim fingerprint on the attack, come 200 or 300 bias incidents. That was a wake-up call," he says. "This is the second one, a kick in the back. This is telling us, `Get your act together or you'll be marginal forever.' "

SHUFFLING through the daily invasion of junk mail became a daily adventure for Dr. Khan, president of the New York State chapter of the American Muslim Alliance, after Mr. Lazio branded $50,000 in contributions to Hillary Rodham Clinton from members in Massachusetts as "blood money." It came from people, Mr. Lazio said, who tacitly supported terrorist acts like that against the destroyer Cole.

If there's guilt by association, this must mean Dr. Khan, a polite and scholarly cardio-pulmonary specialist with a middle-of-the-line Lexus in his driveway and a classic Rolex on his wrist, is tight with various terrorists, too. Even if he deplores the attack on the Cole as "reprehensible." He chooses that same word for Mr. Lazio's recent public statements about Muslim groups.

Will today's mail bring the umpteenth unsolicited request for

156

money for Mr. Lazio's war chest? Will there be a sequel to the anti-Hillary tract that arrived this summer? Or maybe a Lazio bumper sticker to join the one gathering dust upstairs?

Doesn't Mr. Lazio realize that Dr. Khan, a habitual ticket-splitter, is so repulsed by what he calls "all the mud flying around" that he is devoting himself to mobilizing New York's Muslim vote against Mr. Lazio?

"Thank God for the Internet," he exclaims. "The e-mails are flying all over the state."

Dr. Khan, who teaches at the State University of New York at Stony Brook, says his main role with the alliance involves encouraging Muslims to register to vote, not telling them how to vote. But this time he's making an exception.

"Yes, I'm telling them how we think they should vote; it doesn't mean they'll listen," he says. But last week, for the first time, the nation's Muslim groups banded under a single umbrella to endorse a presidential candidate, Gov. George W. Bush. Dr. Khan says that Vice President Al Gore lost his chance at the endorsement because he ignored the Muslim coalition. Dr. Khan finds it curious that Mr. Lazio's outrage over the alliance's June fund-raiser for Mrs. Clinton didn't surface until last week, just after the Muslims endorsed Mr. Bush.

"I think some people are threatened that the Muslims are looking for a seat at the table. Mr. Lazio's position is extremely offensive and we're going to fight it. We're going to fight it at the polls."

Dr. Khan's other fight is equally personal – and, he suspects, political. In 1999, after a dozen years as chairman of the department of medicine at Nassau County Medical Center, he was told his contract would not be renewed. He says there were rumors that his position at the alliance was a factor. "It seems whenever any Muslim gets too high of a profile, this glass ceiling comes down," says Dr. Khan, who has filed a lawsuit accusing the hospital of discrimination and wrongful dismissal. "We'll let the courts decide."

GLOSSARY

Adhan	Call to prayer.
Allah	The Arabic proper name of the One God, the Creator and Lord of the universe, the God of Adam, Noah, Abraham, Moses, Jesus, Muhammad and all the prophets.
Asr	The midafternoon prayer, title of 103rd Sura of the *Holy Quran*.
Assalaamu Alaikum	"Peace be unto you." Used upon greeting and leaving a person.
Ayat	Signs, proofs, clear evidence of miracles; also verses of the *Quran*.
Califa (also Khalifah)	Successor, vicar, lieutenant.
Dawah	Call, appeal, invocation, invitation, supplication, propagation of Islam.
Eid al-Adha	Feast or festival. Muslims have two eids (holidays) – the first celebrating the completion
Eid al-Fitr	the fast of Ramadhan, and the second commemorating Prophet Abraham's obedience to God. Muslims celebrate these eids (holidays) with special congregational prayers, acts of charity and gatherings with family and friends.
Fajr	Dawn; first prayer of the day.
Ghusl	Taking a bath in a religious, ceremonial way.
Hadith	The recorded statements of the Prophet Muhammad memorized and written down by his companions and later compiled in various collections. Of these, Bukhari and Muslims are the two most authentic.
Hafiz	One who has committed the complete *Quran* to memory.
Hajj	A pilgrimage to Mecca which is obligatory for every Muslim who can afford it.
Hijab	Veiling or concealing.
Hijra	Prophet Muhammad's migration from Mecca to Medina, marking year one of the Muslim calendar.
Imam	A responsible, knowledgeable leader who leads others in prayer.
Isha	The night prayer, performed about one-and-one-half hours after sunset.

Islam	Literally, "submission" or surrender. Islam means obedience and submission to God. Islam also means "peace," emphasizing the fact that it is only through obedience to God that man can achieve real peace with himself and with other forms of God's creation around him. Those who believe and practice Islam are Muslims. The *Quran* teaches that all of God's prophets, since the creation of man, were in this sense Muslims, and that their core message to mankind was Islam or the message of peace and obedience to God.
Jihad	An effort or struggle in the cause of God.
Juma (also jumua)	Friday; day of reunion or gathering.
Khutbah	The sermon delivered on Friday before the prayer, Eid prayers, engagement, betrothal.
Maghrib	Sunset prayer.
Masjid (plural, masajid)	Place of prayer; mosque.
Mosque	From the Arabic masjid, "a place of prostration."
Muhammad (also Mohamed, Mohammed)	The Prophet of Islam (570-632)
Qibla	The direction towards which Muslims face during prayers. The first Qibla was Jerusalem, which later on was changed to Mecca.
Quran (also Koran)	The holy book of Islam. It was revealed by Allah (God) in Arabic. Revelation of the *Quran* began during the month of Ramadhan in AD 610. The angel Gabriel appeared with the first revelation, the beginning of *Sura* 96. Unchanged since revelation and considered eternal, the Quran is revered as the divine word of Allah (God) and is recited in every prayer.
Ramadhan	The ninth month of the Islamic calendar.
Sunnah	A path, a way of life, all the traditions and practices of Prophet Muhammad that have become models to be followed by Muslims.
Sura (also Surah)	A row or series, strictly refers to the chapters in the *Quran*.
Taqwah	God consciousness. "Fear of Allah". Self restraint, doing good, avoiding sin, wrong, injustice.
Zuhr	Noon prayer.